To Mike,
   A gifted young man who
consumes books on military
history. Best of luck with
your future plans. Hope these
true stories of Americans at
their best will entertain
and inspire.

                With Best Wishes!
                David Evans
                Christmas 2002

Random Acts of Kindness

True Stories of America's Civil War

Compiled and Edited

by

David Evans

&

Based on an idea by

Tom Broadfoot

BROADFOOT PUBLISHING COMPANY

WILMINGTON
2001

"Fine Books Since 1971."

BROADFOOT PUBLISHING COMPANY

1907 Buena Vista Circle

Wilmington, North Carolina 28411

THIS BOOK IS PRINTED ON ACID-FREE PAPER

ISBN No. 1-56837-392

For Kitty and Ebb,

who have always inspired by example.

Random Acts of Kindness

PREFACE

This is not a book about battles. It does not describe strategy or tactics or try to explain the causes of victory and defeat. It is simply a collection of short stories with one thing in common. They all describe random acts of kindness that took place during America's Civil War.

To the best of my knowledge, these stories are true. Fiction often masquerades as fact, but I have tried to carefully research each selection and weed out those that wither in the glare of close scrutiny. Occasionally, however, I have had to take a leap of faith and rely on the seeming honesty and good intentions of the writer.

I have supplied titles for some stories and changed the titles of others to better suit the purpose of this book. I have also tried to correct spelling, punctuation, and a few factual errors, sometimes adding a word or two for the sake of clarity. The rank given for those authors who served in the Union or Confederate armies is the rank they held at the time the incident took place. Wherever possible, the original source of the story appears below the author's name.

Random Acts of Kindness

INTRODUCTION

"War means fightin' and fightin' means killin'." That was how one Civil War general described the fierce struggle that pitted fathers against sons, brothers against brothers, and claimed the lives of more Americans than World War I, World War II, and the Korean War combined. It was America's darkest hour.

But there was light in that darkness. Even during the carnage at Antietam and the appalling cruelty at Andersonville, there were brief, bright, shining moments when soldiers and civilians on both sides set aside hatred and hostility long enough to perform acts of genuine kindness and compassion. As you are about to see, such incidents were not uncommon, for a number of reasons.

Unlike the combatants in most of America's wars, Billy Yank and Johnny Reb shared a common language. Whether they spoke with a slow Southern drawl or the crisp, clipped sentences of a Connecticut Yankee, the vast majority of Civil War soldiers spoke English and could easily understand each other.

They also shared some common beliefs. As President Abraham Lincoln noted in his second inaugural address, both sides read the same Bible, prayed to the same God, and each invoked His aid against the other. Millions of Americans, North and South, had read and studied the Bible since childhood. They had grown up listening to Sunday morning sermons about the good Samaritan who stopped to help an injured stranger, and how Jesus taught his followers to "Love your enemies," and to "Do unto others as you would have them do unto you."

Like other soldiers in other times, many of the men who shouldered muskets and marched off to war took these lessons with them. Centuries earlier, Christianity had given rise to a code of conduct for medieval knights and men at arms. Chivalry, as this code was called, emphasized honor, fair play, and compassion for the weak and less fortunate. Beginning in 1814, Sir Walter Scott's Waverley novels introduced chivalry's lofty ideals to thousands of American readers, particularly in the South. Just how much impact these romantic tales of gallant knights and ladies fair had on the battlefield behavior of Civil War soldiers is hard to say, but one historian has asserted Scott's widely read novels, such as *Ivanhoe* and *The Talisman*, were "the Bible's only competitors for the attention of literate Southerners."

Another powerful and pervasive influence in Civil War America was Freemasonry. Thousands of members of this mysterious fraternal organization had sworn a solemn oath to practice brotherly love and to help those in need. Regardless of whether he wore Union blue or Confederate gray, a sick or injured Mason who identified himself to a brother Mason could count on getting help.

Not every soldier was a Mason, but combat did create a special camaraderie among friends as well as foes. Billy Yank and Johnny Reb faced common hardships and dangers and shared the same uncertain future. This made all soldiers, no matter which flag they fought for, "brothers in arms."

All of these factors—a common language, shared beliefs, the Biblical teachings of Jesus, the benevolent influences of chivalry and Freemasonry, and the "brotherhood of arms"—made Billy Yank and Johnny Reb more alike than different. This kinship, this shared humanity, often brought out the best in Northerners and Southerners alike. As one Union soldier noted in a letter he wrote from the front lines during the summer of 1864, "There was never before a civil war in which there was so little animosity."

Today we live in a cynical and often self-centered world. Why should anyone care about half forgotten good deeds that happened over a century ago? How can they possibly be relevant now?

I believe these stories have an important lesson to teach us, not only about our past, but also about our future. An unknown, but often quoted, philosopher summed up that lesson with these words: "I looked for the greatness of America in her fields and did not find it there. I looked for the greatness of America in her industries and did not find it there. I looked for the greatness of America in her churches and there I found it. America is great because she is good, and if America ever ceases to be good, she will cease to be great."

David Evans

Random Acts of Kindness

1861

THE CALL TO ARMS

Random Acts of Kindness

When Fort Sumter Surrendered

Almost a fatal accident occurred to Colonel Roger A. Pryor shortly after his arrival at the fort. He was sitting in the hospital at a table, with a black bottle and a tumbler near his right hand. The place was quite dark, having been built up all around with boxes of sand to render it shellproof. Being thirsty and not noticing what he did, he mechanically picked up the bottle, poured some of the liquid into the glass, and drank it down.

It proved to be iodide of potassium, which is quite a poisonous compound. When I saw him, he was very pale and leaning on the shoulder of Dr. Samuel W. Crawford, who was taking him out on the grass to apply the stomach pump. He was soon out of danger.

Some of us questioned the doctor's right to interpose in a case of this kind. It was argued that if any Rebel leader chose to come over to Fort Sumter and poison himself, the medical department had no business to interfere with such a laudable intention. The doctor, however, claimed, with some show of reason, that he himself was held responsible to the United States for the medicine in the hospital, and therefore he could not permit Pryor to carry any of it away.

Captain Abner Doubleday,
1st U.S. Artillery
Reminiscences of Forts Sumter and Moultrie

A Heroine in Baltimore

The band of the 6th Regiment of Massachusetts Volunteers that left Boston in April 1861 consisted of twenty-four persons, who, together with their musical instruments, occupied a car by themselves from Philadelphia to Baltimore. By some accident, the musicians' car got switched off at the Canton Depot, so that, instead of being the first, it was left in the rear of all the others.

After the mob had attacked the soldiers, they came upon the car in which the band was still sitting, wholly unarmed, and incapable of making any defense. The infuriated demons approached them howling and yelling, and poured in upon them a shower of stones, broken iron, and other missiles, wounding some severely, and demolishing their instruments. Some of the miscreants jumped upon the roof of the car, and with a bar of iron beat a hole through it, while others were calling for powder to blow them all up in a heap.

Finding that it would be sure destruction to remain longer in the car, the poor fellows jumped out to meet their fiendish assailants hand to hand. They were saluted with a shower of stones, but took to their heels, fighting their way through the crowd, and running at random, without knowing in what direction to go for assistance or shelter.

As they were hurrying along, a rough-looking man suddenly jumped in front of their leader and exclaimed, "This way, boys! This way!"

It was the first friendly voice they had heard since entering Baltimore, and they stopped to ask no questions, but followed their guide, who took them up a narrow court, where they found an open door, into which they rushed, being met inside by a powerful-looking woman, who grasped each one by the hand and directed them upstairs. The last of their band was knocked senseless just as he was entering the door, by a stone, which struck him on the head; but the woman who had welcomed them immediately caught up their fallen comrade and carried him in her arms up the stairs.

"You are perfectly safe here, boys," said the Amazon, who directly proceeded to wash and bind up their wounds.

After having done this, she procured them food and then told them to strip off their uniforms and put on the clothes she had brought them, a motley assortment of baize jackets, ragged coats, and old trousers. Thus equipped, they were enabled to go out in search of their companions, without danger of attack from the Plug Uglies and Blood Tubs, who had given them so rough a reception.

They then learned the particulars of the attack upon the soldiers, and of their escape, and saw lying at the station the two men who had been killed, and the others who had been wounded. One of their own band was missing, and he has not yet been found, and it is uncertain whether he was killed or not.

On going back to the house where they were so humanely treated, they found that their clothes had been carefully tied up, and with their battered instruments, had been sent to the depot of the Philadelphia Railroad, where they were advised to go themselves. . . .

The noble-hearted woman who rescued these men is a well-known character in Baltimore and, according to all the usages of Christian society, is an outcast and a polluted being; but she is a true heroine, nevertheless, and entitled to the grateful consideration of the country. When Maryland Governor Thomas H. Hicks had put himself at the head of the rabble rout of miscreants, and Congressman Henry Winter Davis had fled in dismay, and the men of wealth and official dignity had hid themselves in their terror, and the police were powerless to protect the handful of unarmed strangers who were struggling with the infuriated mob, this degraded woman took them under her protection, dressed their wounds, fed them at her own cost, and sent them back to the safety of their homes.

As she is too notorious in Baltimore not to be perfectly well known by what we have already told of her, it will not be exposing her to any persecution to mention her name. Ann Manley is the name by which she is known in the city of Blood Tubs, and the loyal men of the North, when they march again through its streets, should remember her for her humanity to their countrymen.

The Civil War in Song and Story

A Chivalrous Soldier

War must always be terrible, but it need not be unrelieved by shining examples of chivalry and consideration for others as well as by the display of courage and self-sacrifice that are inseparable from it. Our own War Between the States was full of such amenities between the warring soldiers. One of the most charming courtesies was shown by Brigadier General Irvin McDowell, who commanded the Federal troops at Bull Run, to the wife of General Robert E. Lee.

On May 24, 1861, a column of Federal troops from Washington took possession of Arlington Heights and Alexandria. The family of General Lee left the beautiful Arlington mansion as the troops approached. Subsequently the Federal commander, Major General Charles W. Sandford, was relieved by General McDowell, and it was into the latter's hands that a letter from Mrs. Lee addressed to the commander at Arlington fell.

General McDowell's reply is as follows:

Headquarters
Department of Northeastern Virginia,
Arlington, May 30, 1861.

Mrs. R. E. Lee
Madam:

Having been ordered by the government to relieve Major General Sandford in command of this department,

I had the honor to receive this morning your letter of today addressed to him at this place.

With respect to the occupation of Arlington by the United States troops, I beg to say it has been done by my predecessor with every regard to the preservation of the place.   I am here temporarily in camp on the grounds, preferring this to sleeping in the house, under the circumstances which the painful state of the country places me with respect to its proprietors.

I assure you it has been and will be my earnest endeavor to have all things so ordered that on your return you will find things as little disturbed as possible. In this I have the hearty concurrence of the courteous, kind-hearted gentleman in the immediate command of the troops quartered here, and who lives in the lower part of the house to insure its being respected.

Everything has been done as you desired with respect to your servants, and your wishes, as far as they are known or could be anticipated, have been complied with. When you desire to return, every facility will be given you for so doing.

I trust, madam, you will not consider it an intrusion if I say I have the most sincere sympathy for your distress and that, as far as is compatible with my duty, I shall always be ready to do whatever may alleviate it. I have the honor to be, very respectfully, your most obedient servant,

Irvin McDowell.

P.S. —I am informed it was the order of the General-in-Chief, if the troops on coming here found the family in the house that no one should enter it, but that a guard should be placed for its protection.

Compiled from
Confederate Veteran
and
Official Records of the Union and Confederate Armies

A Woman's Prerogative

The 21st of July, 1861, on which the first battle of Bull Run took place, was an exceedingly hot day; at least it appeared to be so by all who had not been accustomed to violent exercise in a warm climate. On the way to the battleground in the morning, before reaching Sudley Church, I went up to a large white house, at one of the windows of which a lady was standing, watching the passing troops, and I politely asked for some water. She gave me a gruff and insolent answer, and I turned away with feelings not the kindliest imaginable.

On our way back in the afternoon, after our signal defeat, I saw the same lady standing at the same window, with a tin cup in her hand, from which she was dispensing water to a goodly sized crowd of our thirsty men. I rode through the crowd and asked her for a drink. She passed the cup to me with very little water in it, and I found it deliciously cold and refreshing. As she handed me the cup, she remarked, "I can only give this to the wounded, for my ice is almost out, and I want very much to look out for them."

My acrimonious feelings on the morning were entirely dispelled, for her heart, stubborn with the well and strong, had melted to the most kindly sympathy with those whose sufferings required a refreshing draught, though they were enemies to the cause she evidently was devoted to.

And in this connection I will say, it was my experience throughout the war, that the women invariably by acts and words, disclosed their sympathy for one side or the other without fear or hesitation, while the men, as a rule, palavered and manifested a sort of I-must-scratch-your-back air.

Lieutenant J. Albert Monroe,
Reynolds' Rhode Island Battery
MOLLUS Papers

Captured at Wilson's Creek

I was captured with four other commissioned officers and about forty enlisted men. After our capture we were reconducted to the battlefield, arriving there near sundown. We were permitted to drink water, lying down at the edge of the creek, and then taken to a field of wheat stubble; there were gathered about two hundred men, nearly all from General Franz Sigel's column. . . .

The day had been very hot, and the night was very cold, owing to the altitude of the Ozark Mountains, and as we possessed no blankets, we were saturated with dew, and real glad when on Sunday, August 11th, old Sol made his appearance. Till Sunday afternoon the Texas cavalry which had captured us remained as our guard, but Sunday afternoon it was relieved by the 3rd Louisiana Infantry, who conducted us to a new camp about two miles from the first location and near the headquarters of General Nicholas B. Pearce, who commanded the Arkansas troops of General Ben McCulloch's army.

In the evening General Pearce made his appearance in our camp, and seeing some officers with shoulder straps—Lieutenants Gustavus A. Schaffer and Charles Mann of Sigel's artillery—he asked them if there were any more officers, and we were all pointed out to him; when he told us that if we would give our word of honor that we would make no attempt to escape, he would invite us to a supper at his headquarters. We gave our word and accepted his invitation with thanks, for we had had nothing to eat since Friday.

It kept several Negro servants busy to bring victuals owing to their rapid disappearance. At the table we were joined by two officers of a Kansas volunteer regiment, and while we were eating, Colonel James McIntosh, the adjutant general of General McCulloch appeared, and we were introduced to him by name. He told us that we could have the liberty of the whole camp if we would give him our word of honor that we would make no attempt to escape, which we readily did.

On Monday morning, having spent the night at General Pearce's headquarters, the general's table supplied us with a breakfast, and at noon Colonel McIntosh called for us to take us to the headquarters of General McCulloch. Thanking General Pearce (a West Point graduate, and former first lieutenant of the regular army) for his great kindness, we followed Colonel McIntosh. . . .

When we arrived at McCulloch's headquarters, Colonel McIntosh introduced us to him, one after another, and he cordially shook hands with every one of us. Then he informed us that he intended to take his troops back to Arkansas, Missouri not belonging to the Confederate States, and he would have to turn us over to General Sterling Price. Lieutenant Colonel Anselm Albert, of the 3rd Missouri Infantry, informed General McCulloch that it would be impossible for him to walk to Springfield, (twelve miles) as he suffered from a severe contusion of his right hip from a shrapnel ball, whereupon General McCulloch said, "Gentlemen, you can take my four-mule ambulance."

This we gratefully accepted. Arriving at Springfield, we reported to General Price, who had established his headquarters at the Chambers Hotel. Aligning us on the west wall of the hotel parlor, he counted noses and then addressed us as follows: "Gentlemen, I presume you don't wish to be confined, and if you give me your word of honor that you will not attempt to escape you can select any vacant house in town and report here in person every morning at nine o'clock."

We gave our word and quartered ourselves in a vacant house near our old camp. Being the youngest officer, I was made commissary, and returning to General Price, told him that we had nothing to eat and asked to have some rations issued to us. The general directed his adjutant, Colonel Thomas L. Snead, to give us an order on the Commissary Department for rations.

Walking across the public square, I found the commissary general of the Missouri State Guard, established in a store, all the goods having been confiscated and designated as hospital stores. The gentleman had been a member of Congress, but abandoned his seat to fight for the Confederacy. He received me very cordially and said, "Boys, I will give you the best I have got, and if you catch me, treat me the same way." He kept his word and gave us an abundance—even smoking tobacco, for I had a six months' supply when I returned to my regiment.

Every morning at nine o'clock we reported to General Price, and on Sunday, the 18th of August, he addressed us as follows: "Gentlemen, would you like to go back to St. Louis?"

We assured him we would.

"Well," he said, "if you will sign your parole, not to bear arms against either the state of Missouri or the Confederate States of America, you can go home, but you have to leave my camp inside of twenty-four hours."

Next morning, August 19th, we signed a parole in duplicate, one copy we got, and one copy Colonel Snead retained. I well remember the day, for it was my twentieth birthday.

On our march to Carthage, in July, we had been joined by a man who had a farm two miles from Springfield. He had been a freighter, carting goods from Rolla, Missouri, the terminus of the

Southwest Branch of the Pacific Railroad, to Springfield, a distance of one hundred and twenty miles. He went with us from Springfield to Carthage and back, as an assistant wagon master, he being a Union man, while his two boys were in Price's army. He offered to take us to Rolla in two wagons if we paid him sixty dollars. This we agreed to, and he took us out to his farm the same day, lodging us overnight and starting for Rolla bright and early Tuesday, August 20th. We were eight commissioned officers and one enlisted man, who was a friend from St. Louis, and later became first lieutenant and quartermaster of the 24th Illinois. Our old freighter knew everybody living along the road, and made it a point to always stop for the night at the house of a Union man, of which there were plenty in southwest Missouri.

Everything went well until the afternoon of the second day, when about four miles west of Lebanon, Missouri, we were met by a dozen fellows, who were going to Springfield, to join Price's army. They were well mounted and armed with rifles, shotguns, pistols, and bowie knives. They halted our wagons and wanted to know who we were. They were not drunk, but had whiskey enough in them to make them very ugly.

We explained to them that we were officers on parole going back to St. Louis and showed them our written paroles. After some consultation, the leader, a strapping Missourian, said, "Get out of the wagons, you damned Dutch sons of female dogs, and get in line alongside the road and then you hurrah for Jeff Davis, or you die!"

They being heavily armed, and we possessing nothing but pocketknives, of course we complied with their polite request, but refused to hurrah for Jeff Davis and argued the case with them. Our spokesman was Second Lieutenant Gustavus A. Finklenburg of the 1st Missouri Infantry. . . . Finklenburg was a young St. Louis attorney and pleaded eloquently. . . .

Things were rapidly approaching a tragedy; those Missouri scoundrels were getting their shooting irons ready to execute their threat, when at the nearest bend of the road, east of us, appeared a buggy drawn by two mules, a little mulatto boy driving, and a gray-coated officer sitting in it. As the buggy rapidly approached, we recognized the officer as Captain Emmett MacDonald, whom we had captured at Camp Jackson, St. Louis, Missouri, on May 10th. He was the only officer who refused to give his parole and was released by the United States District Court on a writ of habeas corpus, while the others all gave their parole and many of them broke it.

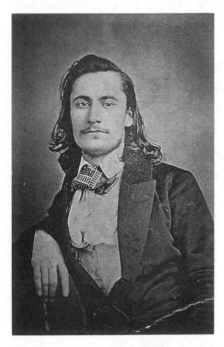

Captain Emmett MacDonald

Captain MacDonald was a young St. Louis attorney and cordially greeted Lieutenant Finklenburg as a brother lawyer. When Finklenburg had explained the situation to him, he reached under the buggy seat and pulled out two Colt navy revolvers, cocked them, and pointing them at our valiant captor, he said, "Boys, I am Captain Emmett MacDonald of General Price's staff. The first one of you who touches a hair on the head of any of these gentlemen, I will kill him like a dog. Now, go on to Springfield and get away from here!" and our captors slunk away like whipped dogs. After fervently thanking Captain MacDonald, for he had undoubtedly saved our lives, we proceeded on our journey.

Poor Captain MacDonald was a brother of the celebrated sculptor, James Wilson Alexander MacDonald. He wore his hair very long and had made a vow not to have it cut until the Confederacy had been established. Alas, he fell with his uncut hair at the battle of Hartville, Missouri, in January 1863. We arrived at Rolla on Friday, August 23rd, at about 2:00 p.m., and, oh, the joy we felt when we had placed a vidette of two United States cavalrymen between ourselves and the Confederate States of America.

Captain Otto C. B. Cademann,
3rd Missouri (Union) Infantry
MOLLUS Papers

A Philadelphia Welcome

A soldier of the 4th New Hampshire Regiment gives his experience in Philadelphia as follows:

We arrived in the city at five o'clock on Sunday morning, September 29, 1861, and the regiment was welcomed in a matter better appreciated than described. Within five or six rods of the ferry are three or four hundred washbowls, with pipes of warm and cold water to supply them. Here a scene followed, which reminded me that "cleanliness is next to godliness." Then we were marched to a building literally filled with nice bread, hot coffee, cold meats, pickles, cheese, and sauerkraut and invited to partake of a Quaker's hospitality. After eating we were informed that stationery and every convenience for writing was at our disposal, and not a few accepted the kind privilege of writing home. No pay would be received for postage stamps, which were furnished as freely as water.

As the good old matrons, with their three-cornered handkerchiefs and nicely ironed caps, glided among us, attending our every want, inquiring after our health, wishing us Godspeed, etc., many an eye was moistened, and emotions awakened, which, perhaps, had been sleeping in many for years. And as the Quaker girls shook our hands, and even kissed some of the Yankee boys, I know our New Hampshire girls will not be jealous if we say, and truthfully, too, that for the time being we forgot them at home. Although it is said that on one or two occasions "the Quakers didn't come out," it is true they come out to meet every regiment that passes through their city in a manner that no other city can boast of.

The Civil War in Song and Story

The Old Man and the Private

In the early part of the war I was a private soldier, under Stonewall Jackson, in Virginia. At that time I was a mere boy, and my gun was almost as big and heavy as I was. You can imagine how tired and hungry I was after I had marched two days without any food. A driving rainstorm came on, and I could hardly drag my feet along the muddy road.

A tent by the roadside attracted my attention, and I saw a gray-bearded face peeping out at the marching troops.

"Hello, old man!" I shouted; "got anything to eat in there?"

"Yes; what's the matter?" the man in the tent replied.

I told him that I was hungry and had been marching two days without a scrap of food.

"Come right in," said the old fellow, pleasantly.

Into the tent I plunged in a hurry, throwing down my gun and smacking my lips in anticipation of a square meal.

The stranger opened a camp chest and invited me to help myself. You should have seen the way I sailed into the rations. I ate ravenously, without saying a word, and for the time forgot all about my kind host.

Finally, he asked me if I would have a drink of water, and handed me a gourd from a bucket in one corner of the tent. I took a big drink and got ready to depart.

"You have been very kind to me," I said to my new friend, "and I would like to know your name."

"My name is Lee," was the answer.

"Lee—what Lee?" I asked him—"not General Lee?"

"That is my name," was his quiet response.

Well, I was taken aback, of course; but I was young and cheeky, and I made the best of it. Soldiers had no handkerchiefs, so I wiped my hands on my breeches and gave the general's paw a cordial shake.

He asked me my name and told me to take care of myself as I left. . . .

That is the story of my meeting with Bob Lee. Do you wonder that we boys all took a fancy to him? He was . . . the Confederacy's grandest chieftain—the idol of the people, the father of his soldiers—royal old Bob Lee!

Private Henry H. Smith
1st Tennessee Infantry
Camp-Fires of the Confederacy

Random Acts of Kindness

1862

FORWARD INTO BATTLE

Random Acts of Kindness

Stonewall's Way

While at Rye Cove, Virginia, I became acquainted with one of Stonewall Jackson's men. . . . The name of this soldier was George Mullen, who was then at home at Rye Cove on sick furlough. As I now remember, he was in General Jackson's old brigade and in the battle of Bull Run, where Jackson's men stood like a stone wall.

The incident occurred on one of General Jackson's rapid flank movements, that were so rapidly executed as to take the enemy by surprise. Mullen said that General Jackson was executing one of his rapid movements in the latter part of winter. The streams were swollen and were covered with soft ice and his regiment was in front. They came to one of those icy streams. The officer in advance rode haughtily to the stream and ordered the men to go forward. The foot soldiers hesitated to go into the cold water. This offended this martinet, and he rode to the water's edge with drawn sword and said he would run them through if they again halted. This was like a firebrand. The soldiers became so enraged that it seemed they would take him from his horse and tear him to pieces. Other officers came up and ordered the men into the water. One of them said that if they disobeyed again he would order up a battery and fire into them. This only increased the fury of the men, and the officers had lost control of the troops.

Just then Stonewall Jackson came to the front. Some of the officers rode back rapidly to meet him. General Jackson waved them aside and leisurely rode to the front. He observed a young soldier whose feet were almost bare, and so footsore that he was lame; besides, he was hoarse from the effects of measles.

General Jackson thus addressed this boy soldier, "Son, why are you not back at the hospital?"

The lad replied, "General, I did not join the army to fill a hospital bunk, but to do a soldier's duty."

Then General Jackson dismounted and told the young soldier to mount his horse and ride across the stream. The boy objected, saying he was not worthy to ride while his commander was afoot. General Jackson walked to the water's edge and in a quiet voice said, "Come on, boys," when the soldiers gave a loud cheer and waded the stream in perfect order. Many of the officers, having been thus rebuked by their commander, put the most disabled men on their horses and followed their leader.

1862

Southern soldiers could not be driven like hirelings, but would go to sure death in obedience to their commander, whom they loved, and who had shown in so many ways that he was willing to endure the privations and hardships with his soldiers. . . .

Orderly Sergeant George D. Ewing,
4th Kentucky Cavalry
Confederate Veteran

The Amenities of War

It was Sunday, the first day of the battle of Shiloh, the first engagement of the 2nd Texas Infantry Regiment. The regiment had entered the battle on the right-center of the Confederate line, which had pressed back the Federal forces in its front until about three o'clock in the afternoon. After making a desperate charge across a running branch, where the killed and wounded of both sides thickly bestrewed the hillside, and we had made a lodgment on the crest of a hill that terminated on our right in a bluff overlooking the Tennessee River, and had halted to rest and rally our forces, Dan Smith and I were sent to the rear with the canteens of our company to fill them with water. The sun of that April evening was sweltering hot, as is often the case before a rain. On our way down the hill, we passed many dead bodies of Federal soldiers, when our attention was attracted by the groans of one poor fellow in the uniform of a captain, who lay with one leg pressed out of shape under him. We approached him and asked if we could do anything for his relief.

He replied that he would be grateful to us if we would straighten him out, as his leg was badly shot to pieces, and the pain was almost killing him. Another man lying near him desired water, and a third complained of the burning sun. We raked some dry leaves into a bed under the sheltering boughs of a neighboring tree, and placing the captain on it, asked what else we could do for his comfort.

He then asked if we would not place the other two men, who were members of his company, beside him, so that they might be able to assist each other. We enlarged the bed of leaves and placed the other two men on it by his side. In placing the captain in position, I observed that he wore a heavy gold watch-guard which extended around his neck. I suggested that he had better allow me to take it off and put it in his pocket, as some plunderer might come along and rob him of it. He insisted that I should take it off and keep it, saying, "I am sure I cannot recover, and I wish you to keep it for your kindness to us."

This I declined to do, but took the watch and guard and put them into his pocket. Then we took their canteens with our own to the branch and filled them with water, and on the way picked up some well-filled haversacks, and on returning placed these with the filled canteens by their sides.

The three were profuse in their expressions of gratitude and asked us to write our names in their memorandum books, which we did. In returning their books, and on their reading our names with that of our regiment, "2nd Texas Infantry," they looked at us in astonishment and asked if we were really Texans. When we assured them we were, they said they were astonished, for they had prayed not to fall into the hands of Texans, as they believed that if they did, they would be shown no quarter and would certainly be butchered like beasts. . . .

To these remarks, I replied, "Did we fight you like men? And are not the brave always kind?"

They answered, "You fought more like demons than like men; but surely your kindness cannot be questioned, and we cannot express our gratitude for it."

Just then we saw in the woods nearby an ambulance of our corps. Hailing it and placing them in it, we sent them to the rear.

They were of the Illinois troops, and, if I mistake not, the captain's name was Miller.

After this the 2nd Texas passed through the battles of Farmington, Iuka, Corinth, Hatchie Bridge, Chickasaw Bayou, and Fort Pemberton, and then was engaged in the siege of Vicksburg.

On the night of . . . the last day of May, about midnight, a false alarm aroused us to arms, and in a moment the sleeping lines became a blaze of fire from the throats of muskets and artillery, and the air groaned with the shrieks of shell and the whirring of "Minnies." Amidst the aimless firing, a ten-inch shrapnel exploded in the trench where I stood, and three of its pieces found lodgment in my form, one severing my left foot from the ankle, another grazing my left hip and lodging against my right hip joint, whilst the third grazed my backbone and lodged against my right shoulder blade.

I was borne by my faithful comrades through the rain of lead and iron that deluged the battlefield to the surgeon; and after this through the remainder of the forty-seven days of the conflict, endured a struggle for life against the intense summer heat, flying death-missiles, starvation, maggots, and inexpressible pain until the surrender came. My brave and true comrades filed into my tent at the hospital, and with solemn mien and bowed heads and smothered "good-byes," laid half of their small supply of coin on my couch, and with warm press of hand and hushed "God bless you," left me, as they thought, forever.

All the wounded who were unable to go out of the city were concentrated into one hospital in the old Vick mansion on the hill, where they were under the supervision of a Federal surgeon and the surveillance of a Federal guard. My spirits ran low and my lifeblood ebbed and flowed with feverish excitement as I thought, "There is not a friend that I know or a hand that will lovingly help me," when a guard, who paced the old mansion hall, halted at the door of the ward where I lay and asked if there were any Texas soldiers in the room.

John Derbanne, who lay on a cot by the door, replied that there was.

"Are there any of the 2nd Texas Infantry here, do you know?"

Derbanne replied that there was and pointed to my bed.

He approached me and asked, "Do you belong to the 2nd Texas Infantry?"

I answered, "I do."

"Were you in the battle of Shiloh?"

"I was."

"Did your regiment wear white Negro cloth clothes in that battle?"

"It did."

His rifle butt came down on the floor with a thump, and from his shirt pocket, with a hasty twist and a surge, he drew a worn and blackened memorandum book with leaves well gone, and turning to a page in it with nervous hand, he thrust it before my eyes and said, "Do you know the men whose names are written there?"

My eyes and arms were weak and uncertain, but adjusting the book as best I could to the focus of my eyes, I replied, "I do; the first name is mine, the other Dan Smith's, of my company."

His lips quivered. There was a sudden choking in his throat; his sturdy form trembled, as with husky voice he asked, "Do you know me?"

"I do not."

"Did you write that?"

"That's my handwriting."

"D'you remember picking up three men an' putting 'em on a bed of leaves in th' shade, an' giv'n 'em water 'n' something to eat, an' tak'n' a watch off'n the cap'n an' puttin' it in his pocket, an' then put'n' 'em in an amb'lance an' send'n' off to th' hospital?"

"Yes."

"I'm one of 'em."

The tears flowed down his iron cheek. His form of battle-steel was convulsed with nervous emotion. His sturdy arms clasped my emaciated form to his convulsing bosom, which had braved bayonet and shot and shell unflinchingly on many a field of carnage, and I felt serenely secure in my enemy's embrace. A hero's tears fell on my face and were mingled with my own. With dallying reluctance I was released from his embrace, and then with sobbing utterance he gasped, "You saved my life and that of my captain and comrade, and I have hunted for you or some of your command on every battlefield since, that I might prove myself as true to you. Now, what can I do for you? I am ready to do anything under God's heaven that I can."

"Nothing," I replied.

"But I must do something. Do you need money? (His well-filled purse now in his hand.) You must, for you are in our lines now and your money is worthless."

"No, no, I have plenty of money, gold and silver, given me by my comrades when they left me."

"Well, you need clothing?"

"No, I cannot sit up; and though my clothes were torn to shreds when I was wounded, I have no need of others than I have until I am able to be up, which will doubtless be many months yet."

"Tell me how you are wounded."

I told in an ear not less sympathetic than a brother's how I had been smitten by three pieces of shell at one time in the night, and had been borne to the hospital; how there exposed to dangers almost, if not quite, equal to those of the trenches; how the hospital being only supplied with one nurse to ten patients—one half of whom were on duty at a time, in order that the other half might get needed rest—they could not give us proper attention; and how in spite of their best efforts the maggot fly would light on every damp spot on bed or clothing, and flying away would leave, scampering from the spot, numerous, almost microscopic maggots, which would find lodgment in any crease of the skin, broken or not, and eat its way into the flesh; and had eaten between my helpless fingers, behind my ears, and in the creases of my neck, as well as in my wounds, and from the latter had been picked one by one with forceps by a faithful nurse; how with the demands of three large wounds to feed, my system had cried for food and had struggled with starvation; how my bones at knee and hip and shoulder had cut through the skin, and for more than a month I had been compelled to lie on these, burning as with the fires of torment, because I could lie in no other position; how in all this time I had never been dejected or cast down until the surrender had come, and my friends had gone out from me, and with them all hope for the cause for which I had proudly suffered, being able to do no more.

"Are the surgeons kind to you?" he asked.

"Yes, they are. Everyone is kind to me."

"They will be kinder and better still when I have told them who you are and what you did for me. How strange it is that we should meet again with our circumstances so reversed! I have never forgotten your kindness or your face, but you look so young—so much like a mere boy. You were a man when we met each other at Shiloh."

"Yes, I have lost my hair and my beard since I was wounded; all came out, and this new, short hair and beard makes me look young."

"But you need better food than you get here?"

"No, we are all well fed and cared for now. Since General McPherson has been made commandant, he treats us well."

"I must bring in some of our officers and tell them who you are, and hereafter you will be well treated; I know you will."

He then disappeared, but soon reappeared, and with him the Federal surgeon in charge of the Confederate hospital, a colonel and others, to whom this strange tale of another day and this was told. They pledged their undivided attention to the foe that lay there all shattered and torn, and their pledge was not broken, and many of my crippled comrades shared the kindness thus betokened.

Again he was gone, again returned and laid upon my bed tobacco, canned fruit, and many delicacies. He imagined there was not sufficient bedding, and had fresh new blankets, sheets and pillowslips supplied.

At sunset, guard relief came on, an affectionate "good-night" was spoken, and hopes expressed of meeting again on the morrow.

The morrow has not come as yet, but may it not be, if that good day when wars are not, we'll meet again—foe-friends, Johnny Reb and Blue Johnny?

Lieutenant Sterling Fisher,
2nd Texas Infantry
Under Both Flags

Dr. J. A. Derbanne, Washington, La.: "I would like to learn the fate of Sterling Fisher, a lieutenant of the Second Texas Infantry, who was wounded at Vicksburg, and from whom I parted at Shreveport in the latter part of 1863. His home then, I believe, was Houston, Tex. Will appreciate any information about him."

On Shiloh's Bloody Field

The lines were established for the night . . . at a point that had been fiercely fought over during the two days. . . . The wounded had nearly all been carried to the rear, but the ground around us was thickly strewn with the dead. . . .

A cold rain fell continually. Every thread of our clothing was saturated, and we were chilled to the very marrow. Our teeth chattered, and every muscle quivered. . . . Blankets and overcoats— our own had been left back the previous day—were gathered from the field. They were stripped from the dead, who needed them no longer, to cover and warm the living. Three or four men would stand together, or squat upon the muddy ground, throw a blanket soaked with water over their heads, and thus by close contact seek to infuse into each other a little warmth. . . . It was a night that put patience, patriotism, and physical endurance to the severest test. . . .

During the evening, . . . I witnessed an incident that has always remained in my memory. At the foot of a large tree reclined a Rebel soldier, mortally wounded. He was unconscious, and apparently at his last gasp. He was covered with a United States blanket, which some sympathetic friend or foe had thrown over him. Two soldiers in blue stood near, *waiting for him to die* to get his blanket.

"I wish he would die if he is going to!" said one of the shivering men.

They were not hard-hearted enough to take it while the poor man was alive, even though he had been an enemy. An hour later I passed that way again and the blanket was gone. I bent over the motionless form. The man was dead. These true tales sound strangely enough now. . . . But such things, thousands of them, happened on the great battlefields of the war.

Sergeant Wilbur F. Hinman,
65th Ohio Infantry
The Story of the Sherman Brigade

He Was a Child

Two days after the battle of Shiloh I walked into the hospital tent on the ground where the fiercest contest had taken place, and where many of our men and those of the enemy had fallen. The hospital was exclusively for the wounded Rebels, and they were laid thickly around. Many of them were Kentuckians, of General John C. Breckinridge's command.

As I stepped into the tent and spoke to someone, I was addressed by a voice, the childish tone of which arrested my attention: "That's General Rousseau! General, I knew your son Dickey. Where is Dick? I knew him very well."

Turning to him, I saw stretched on the ground a handsome boy about sixteen years of age. His face was a bright one, but the hectic glow and flush on the cheeks, his restless manner, and his gasping and catching his breath as he spoke alarmed me. I knelt by his side and pressed his fevered brow with my hand and would have taken the child into my arms, if I could.

"And who are you, my son?" said I.

"Why, I am Eddy McFadden, from Louisville," was the reply. "I know you, General, and I know your son Dick. I've played with him. Where is Dick?"

I thought of my own dear boy, of what might have befallen him; that he, too, deluded by villains, might, like this poor boy, have been mortally wounded, among strangers, and left to die. My heart bled for the poor child, for he was a child; my manhood gave way, and burning tears attested, in spite of me, my intense suffering. I asked him of his father. He had no father. Your mother? He had no mother. Brothers and sisters?

"I have a brother," said he. "I never knew what soldiering was. I was but a boy, and they got me off down here."

He was shot through the shoulder and lungs. I asked him what he needed. He said he was cold and the ground was hard. I had no tent nor blankets; our baggage was all in the rear. . . . But I sent the poor boy my saddle blanket, and returned the next morning with lemons for him and the rest; but his brother, in the 2nd Kentucky Regiment, had taken him over to his regiment to nurse him. I never saw the child again. He died in a day or two. Peace to his ashes. I never think of this incident that I do not fill up as if he were my own child.

Brigadier General Lovell H. Rousseau
Moore's *Rebellion Record*

As You Sow

Every survivor of the little army known as "General Banks' Division" will always remember the many charming beauties of Virginia's Shenandoah Valley, as it appeared in the spring of 1862. To this division was given the favored privilege of being the first Union troops to march into Winchester and up the valley as far as Harrisonburg. . . .

General Banks' army consisted of two divisions, commanded by Generals Alpheus S. Williams and James Shields. We had almost constant daily skirmishes with the enemy, consisting of General Stonewall Jackson's forces, Colonel Turner Ashby's cavalry acting as their rear guard.

On April 17th the advance was continued from Woodstock, through Edenburg and Mount Jackson, to New Market, the enemy burning bridges and in every way trying to impede the progress of our troops. At Mount Jackson, a scene of destruction presented itself. Here was the terminus of the Manassas Gap Railroad, and the engine house, railroad engines, passenger and freight cars were found in ruins, burned by the Confederates in their retreat to prevent their falling into our hands.

The advance was continued, and on April 25th the division . . . entered Harrisonburg, with colors waving and bands playing national airs. Captain Erwin A. Bowen, of the 28th New York, having been ordered to act as provost marshal on our arrival in Harrisonburg, had obtained permission to march his company—

who were to act as provost guard—in advance of the brigade. We followed the cavalry, which led the division, and thus had the honor of being the first Federal infantry organization to enter Harrisonburg. . . .

Captain Bowen was a model soldier and could never be other than a perfect gentleman: a man of fine physique, tall and erect, with black hair, quick, flash-

ing eyes, and a commanding voice that inspired his men with the same enthusiasm that controlled himself. Quick, sharp, and sometimes stern when in the active command of his company, in the quiet of tent life he was charming. He was one of our best disciplinarians and as a drillmaster had no equal in the regiment. When off duty, no one could be kinder or more approachable. . . . The mem-

Captain Erwin A. Bowen

bers of his company had loved him as a friend and soon learned to admire him as a brilliant soldier. We were proud of our captain, and he always spoke of his company in words of highest praise. . . .

Captain Bowen addressed himself at once to the difficult task of the provost marshal's office with energy and spirit and a conscientious purpose to do his duty without fear or favor. The citizens were assured they would not be molested, but protected in all their rights; guards were placed in every part of the town, and the streets and alleys cleaned; the post office was opened, printing presses started, and every saloon closed. It is said by citizens still living, who were there in 1862, that the good order preserved was fully equal to that maintained in times of peace. The testimony is very general that "Your men were the most gentlemanly that ever occupied the town." Not a drunk soldier was to be seen on the streets, and we had emphatically a temperance place. On the two Sundays we occupied the town, the churches were opened as usual, many soldiers uniting with the citizens in divine worship.

At first the citizens were very much alarmed. They had the natural prejudice against the Yankee soldiers and had become so frightened that many had deserted their homes, while others, if they saw our entry into the place at all, must have done so from behind drawn curtains or closed blinds, as few persons were to be seen. They had little respect for our army, which had come into their midst declaring martial law and taking forcible possession of their town, and had naturally feared our visit would be one of pillage.

When they saw the protection given them in life and property, the many special acts of kindness shown them by the provost marshal, and the orderly conduct of the soldiers, they learned that the invading army were actuated by no feelings of hatred or animosity against them as peaceful citizens, but were fighting to save the Union from disruption. They daily became more friendly and soon made the captain's acquaintance. Many had business with him, and all, whether officially or socially, found him uniformly courteous and obliging. He would not allow them to be interfered with in the transaction of their usual business, and any wrongs perpetrated on them were promptly redressed.

Besides these general acts for the protection of their interests, others could be recalled that endeared him to the citizens in an especial manner. A few such will suffice. A citizen had been arrested for some slight cause and started down the valley as a prisoner. It was brought to the captain's notice that this man's wife was very ill and her life in great danger from the excitement of his arrest. Captain Bowen, by unusual effort, procured his release and return to the bedside of his wife, to her great relief and gratitude.

A Confederate officer, Captain E. A. Shands, had been killed outside our lines, in the eastern portion of the county. He had been a resident of Harrisonburg, and his wife, hearing of his death, visited the provost marshal's office to procure, if possible, permission to go and bring in her husband's body for burial in the village cemetery. This, in the exciting times of war, was an unusual request, and it was with great difficulty that the general in command could be persuaded to allow Captain Bowen to grant the permit.

The correspondence between the two officers is said to have been very warm, the general at first returning the paper unsigned, with this question: "Why —— —— do you ask for such an order?" It was returned again by Captain Bowen, with the following endorsement: "I did not enter the service to fight dead men, women, or children."

This time the order came back approved, and the widow was allowed to go on her sad errand, provided by the captain with an escort and ambulance for the return of the body. Thus he showed his humane spirit and kindliness, and each day the respect and gratitude of the citizens for him increased.

In the midst of these pleasant surroundings, the time passed all too quickly, and just as we had become accustomed to our new duties as provost guard, came the sudden order to march; and, to the great surprise of all, we started down the valley instead of in the advance!

Our purpose, however, is to follow the story of the army only so far as it concerns our story. General Banks' division soon became a part of the "Army of Virginia," commanded by General John Pope, and we left the Shenandoah Valley for the vicinity of Culpeper. To the unusual and severe orders of this general, whose "headquarters were in the saddle," we must here refer, as they have much to do with our article.

This western officer had just been transferred, and had introduced himself to the Army of the Potomac by the bombastic address which is so well known—that we must "discard all ideas of lines of retreat, etc."; that under his superior leadership "we should see only the backs of the enemy, as his policy would be one of attack, and not defense." He had evidently not learned the ancient maxim of soldiers, "not to despise your enemy." The sneering tone of this address was considered a reflection on this army's previous history and strategy, and brought upon this general the dislike, if not the contempt, of the soldiers. Many orders especially offensive to the Confederate authorities followed; citizens were to be held responsible for any damage to railroads, etc., in their vicinity; those not taking the oath of allegiance were to be sent South, and if again found within our lines, to be treated as spies and shot; and many others of a like character. Such orders were considered infamous by the Confederate authorities, and in retaliation similar ones were issued by them against any officers captured from General Pope's army, who were to be held as felons and not to receive the usual treatment accorded to prisoners of war.

About the time these orders were published, our division marched out from Culpeper and was soon engaged in the battle of Cedar Mountain. . . . At this battle, Captain Bowen was taken prisoner, with many others of our regiment and brigade, after having bravely borne their part in the unequal contest, in which nearly every line officer of our regiment was either killed, wounded or taken prisoner. . . .

Captain Bowen and other soldiers captured at Cedar Mountain were taken to Richmond and incarcerated in Libby Prison. Soon after arriving there, an order was issued from the Confederate War Department that all officers from General Pope's army, in accordance with the orders previously referred to, should be allowed no intercourse with other prisoners, but be treated as common felons. The captain and the other officers were at once taken to rooms more secure in the prison, had additional guards placed over them, and were also informed that they were not entitled to the benefit of cartel, for parole and exchange as prisoners of war, but were to be held as hostages, and in the event of any citizen being executed by virtue of the orders of General Pope, would be shot—man for man. . . .

Their condition and feelings can be imagined, daily fearing that the order for their execution would be issued. In the midst of this anxiety, the guard one day called for Captain Bowen, of the 28th New York. Surely, this is the first victim, is the thought of all. The captain was brought before Captain Henry Wirz, then in charge of Libby Prison, who handed him the following paper:

H'dqrs Department Henrico
Richmond, Va., September 11, 1862.

Captain Erwin A. Bowen,
C.S. Military Prison.

Sir:

I am instructed by the general commanding this department to inform you that, in consideration of your kind treatment of our citizens while acting as provost marshal at Harrisonburg, the Secretary of War has directed that you be treated as a prisoner of war, to be exchanged at an early day.

Respectfully,
W. S. Winder, A.A.G.

With feelings of gratitude and joy at his release, Captain Bowen tried to find to whom he was indebted for this unusual order. . . . Winder would give no information beyond the fact of the order, and the captain could learn nothing more. . . . Not until long afterwards did he find that this kindness was the result of the action of the citizens of Harrisonburg, but we give the facts here as they have been verified since by some of the participants.

His friends there saw, among a list of prisoners received at Richmond, the name of their former provost marshal, Captain Bowen, and learned that he, as one of General Pope's officers, had been subjected to the retaliatory orders of the Confederate authorities. They had called a meeting, circulated a petition in his behalf—which was signed by many citizens—had appointed a committee to visit Richmond, and, if possible, secure his release on parole and his early exchange. They visited Jefferson Davis, and their mission was successful in securing the above order for the captain's release. . . . Captain Bowen was granted the freedom of Richmond on his parole, which he improved by visiting many places of interest, and in a few days he was exchanged. . . .

Private C. W. Boyce,
28th New York Infantry
Under Both Flags

He Found Her Boy

To show Jackson's great kindness and consideration for even poor and ignorant people, I remember an incident which happened in the Valley of Virginia while the troops were marching up the Valley Turnpike.

As Jackson rode along with his staff, he was accosted by a poor, plain country woman who wanted to know if he was "Mr. Jackson" and if the troops in the road were his "company." She had brought two or three pair of stockings and some little provisions for her son, who, she told General Jackson, was in his "company." The army . . . was of course made up of divisions, brigades, and regiments, and a great many companies, but this woman only knew that her son, "John," belonged to Jackson's "company," and

General "Stonewall" Jackson

she expressed a great deal of surprise when General Jackson told her that he didn't know her boy.

"What," she said, "don't you know John——? He has been with you a year, and I brought him these socks and something to eat." She began to cry bitterly.

Some members of the staff were disposed to laugh, but Jackson stopped them, got down from his horse, and tried to explain to the woman how it was impossible that he should know her son, a simple private in the ranks, but she persisted he must know him, and she must see him, and that she had spent a great deal of time in fixing these things for him. He asked her what county the boy came from. Then he sent for Lieutenant A. S. Pendleton and asked him what companies were in his army from that county. He then sent three or four couriers to each one of the companies from that county, and found the boy and brought him to the woman, who gave him the present she had for him. Jackson probably spent an hour in doing this deed of real charity.

> Dr. Hunter Holmes McGuire,
> General Thomas J. Jackson's staff
> *Southern Historical Society Papers*

An Incident of the Battle of Malvern Hill

A full-grown rabbit had hid itself away in the copse of a fence, which separated two fields near the center and a most exposed portion of the battleground. Rabbits are want to spend the day almost noiselessly, and in seeming dreamy meditation. This one could have had but little thought—if rabbits think—when choosing its place of retreat at early dawn, that ere it was eventide, there would be such an unwanted and ruthless disturbance.

During all the preparations for battle made around its lair during the forenoon, it nevertheless remained quiet. Early, however, in the afternoon, when the rage of battle had fairly begun, and shot and shell were falling thick and fast in all directions, a shell chanced to burst so near Mr. Rabbit's hiding place that he evidently considered it unsafe to tarry longer.

So, frightened almost to death, out he springs into the open field and runs hither and thither with the vain hope of finding a safe retreat. Whichever way it ran, cannons were thundering out their smoke and fire, regiments of men were advancing or changing position, horses galloping here and there, shells bursting, and solid shot tearing up the ground. Sometimes it would squat down and lie perfectly still, when some new and sudden danger would again start it into motion. Once more it would stop and raise itself as high as possible on its hind legs and look all around for some place of possible retreat.

At length a part of the field seemed open, which was in the

direction opposite from where the battle raged most fiercely. Thither it accordingly ran with all its remaining speed. Unobserved by it, however, a regiment was in that direction, held in reserve, and . . . was lying flat on the ground, in order to escape the flying bullets. Ere the rabbit seemed aware, it had jumped into the midst of the men. It could go no farther, but presently nestled down beside a soldier and tried to hide itself under his arms. As the man spread the skirt of his coat over the trembling fugitive in order to insure it all the protection in his power to bestow, he, no doubt, feelingly remembered how much he himself then needed some higher protection, under the shadow of whose arm might be hidden his own defenseless head from the fast multiplying missiles of death scattered in all directions.

It was not long, however, before the regiment was ordered up and forward. From the protection and safety granted, the timid creature had evidently acquired confidence in man—as the boys are wont to say, "had been tamed." As the regiment moved forward to the front of the battle, it hopped along, tame, seemingly, as a kitten, close at the feet of the soldier who had bestowed the needed protection. Wherever the regiment went, during the remaining part of that bloody day and terrible battle, the rabbit kept close beside its new friend. When night came on, and the rage of battle had ceased, it finally, unmolested and quietly, hopped away, in order to find some old and familiar haunts.

Augusta (Ga.) *Chronicle & Sentinel*

The Last Full Measure

I was in the 87th Regiment, New York Volunteers. We had passed through the campaign of the Peninsula. We came from there to join General Pope. We had several days' intermittent fighting around Manassas, Bristow, Catlett's Station, until on the 30th of August, 1862, we were on the field of the second Bull Run.

Along in the afternoon of that day, I was struck with a piece of shell, which necessitated the amputation of both of my lower limbs. The operation was performed under fire. My comrades, placing me upon a stretcher, started to carry me from the field. Fortunes of war were against us, and it was impossible for them to get me away. They carried me into a house and, filling my canteen with water, bade me good-bye, and barely escaped being taken prisoners.

I with others lay in that house for three or four days. Some were lying in the yards. There were 170, I believe, all told.

It was on the fourth day, I think, that I with some others were moved out into the rear and placed in a little tent. Six men lay in the tent, and the six men had had seven legs amputated. We were lying on a rough board floor; not a rag of clothing on; a thin rubber blanket between our bruised and bleeding bodies and the hard floor; a single blanket to cover our nakedness. I was specially favored by reason of the fact that I had a piece of board about as long as your arm set up slanting for a pillow. We were prisoners of war. Our captors had next to nothing to eat themselves, and we, if possible, had less than they.

1862

The Virginia sun poured down its intense heat. Hunger, thirst, flies, maggots, and all the horrible accompaniments were there. A very few men had been left behind to try and take some sort of care of us, but their numbers were sadly deficient. We lay there one day moaning for water, and there was none to bring it to us.

Just at the entrance to our tent lay a poor fellow who was terribly wounded in the left side, mortally wounded as it proved to be. He was a stranger to us and we to him, but it has always seemed to me since, that that man, in spirit at least, was a descendant, and an honored one, of the most gallant knight of old.

He heard our moans, and out beyond under the trees, he saw there lay some worm-eaten apples that had dropped from the branches overhead. Every movement must have been agony unendurable to that man, and yet he clutched at the grass and dragged himself along inch by inch until at last he was within reach of the apples. Picking them from the ground he placed them in the pocket of his blouse, and then, rolling himself around to keep his sound side on the grass, dragged himself back until he lay again at the entrance to our tent. He reached out the apples one by one, and as I lay nearest the entrance, I took them from his hand and passed them along until each one of my unfortunate comrades had one.

I had just set my teeth in the last one he had handed to me, and it tasted to me at that moment sweeter than the nectar of the gods could have done, when I heard an agonized moan at my right, and turning quickly I saw this good Samaritan with his hands clutching, his eyes rolling. He was in the agonies of death. A moment more and it was all over for him on this side of the Great River. That is all. I never knew even his name. In some home they may mourn him yet as missing. Perhaps his bones have been gathered up and in some of our cemeteries they are interred under the designation, "Unknown."

What that man's past life had been, I know not. It may have been wild, and his speech may have been rough. I know that he was unkempt, unshaven, his clothes soiled with dirt and stained with blood; not at all such a picture as you would welcome, at first sight, into your parlor, or at your dining table. But this I have often thought, that in that last act of his he exhibited so much of what I consider the purely Christ-like attribute, that in the day when you and I shall stand before the just Judge, to be judged for what we have been and not for what we may have pretended to be, I would much rather take my chances in the place of a man who had so large an idea of practical Christianity, than in the place of many more pretentious persons I am acquainted with.

> Corporal James Tanner,
> 87th New York Infantry
> *Camp-Fire Sketches and Battle-Field Echoes*

An Act of Kindness Goes Awry

While we were at Iuka, Mississippi, Confederate General Braxton Bragg was at Chattanooga preparing for his advance into Kentucky. In July we began our movement northward, crossing the Tennessee River at Eastport, and until well into August marched and countermarched in the rear of Altamont and McMinnville, in expectation that Bragg would offer battle somewhere between those points and Murfreesboro, it being supposed that Nashville was the object of his movement.

Quite an exciting episode occurred in one of our camps about this time, in which another character, or I might say two of them, came to the front—McNally, the colonel's striker, and the colonel's mare.

Our colonel, Oliver L. Shepherd, had peculiar ideas about the points of his saddle horse. In the first place, it should not be more than fourteen hands high, as, having short legs, he could not easily mount a taller horse. Next, the back should be short, to prevent the turning of the saddle. And lastly, the back should be long, as an infantry field officer rode generally at a walk to secure an easy motion at that gait.

It was not an easy matter to find an animal which combined all these qualities, but the colonel, having found them in his mare, valued her highly, and after trying a number of grooms had found a suitable one in McNally, who until this unlucky day had been all that could be desired.

We were camped in an old peach orchard. The mare was tied with a heavy rope around her neck to a dead peach tree; she had a trick of pulling back, and nothing less than a cable would hold her on such occasions. The men were lying about in the shade, and the camp was quiet as the grave, when the colonel, coming out of his tent and looking about, saw his mare very restive, stamping and switching her tail, and, although it was blazing hot, covered with a blanket.

"McNally!" he called.

"Yis, Colonel."

"What is the matter with the mare? Why have you got that blanket on her this hot day? Go and take it off immediately."

"Yis, Colonel, but I put the blankit on her because them little yaller flies doos be bitin' her widout it."

As they talked, they moved towards the mare, who was now plunging madly and, just as they reached her, gave one tremendous pull, tore the tree up by the roots, and went tearing through the camp, dragging the tree with her.

The colonel stood speechless with astonishment and dismay, but suddenly he clapped his hand to the back of his neck. The situation dawned upon him with painful distinctness. He turned upon McNally.

"You howling idiot," he shouted, "you've tied her in a yaller-jacket's nest!"

Meanwhile, the poor mare, leaving a trail of the "little yaller flies" behind her, and having knocked down about half the tents in camp, brought up near her starting place, got astride the tree, and was squealing and kicking like an insane mule.

The camp was in an uproar. The men, who had turned out under the impression that we were receiving a charge of cavalry, were laughing and shouting, fighting yellow jackets, and dancing about generally in such a manner that a stranger to the reasons of their conduct might have supposed himself among a lot of escaped lunatics. McNally had disappeared. The colonel, beside himself with rage and anxiety for his mare, was performing a war dance, while the yellow jackets, whose nest was in a hollow of the tree near the roots, were still at home to all callers. At last, a man wrapped in a blanket ran up, cut the rope and set the poor animal free, and the camp gradually resumed its quiet.

Lieutenant Henry B. Freeman,
18th U.S. Infantry
MOLLUS Papers

The Price of Freedom

On one occasion in Virginia, General Wade Hampton came upon a Yankee soldier who was taking a bath in a stream, having left his clothes upon the bank. When the general quietly told the man he was his prisoner, the man was dumbfounded, not being aware that the Confederates were near at hand and supposing himself quite secure. He begged and pleaded to be let off, using every argument he could think of.

After amusing himself by his captive's supplications for some time, General Hampton consented to let him go free. At this the man was delighted and most profuse in thanks, and came ashore to put on his clothes. But the general said, "Ah, no; I can't let you have them. My men are too much in need of clothes. I can't spare them."

After fruitless entreaties the Yankee soldier finally left for his camp as naked as when he was born, and the last words heard from him were, "I'll name my first son Wade Hampton."

Many years after this, as the then Senator Hampton stepped into an elevator in a hotel in Washington, a young man said to him, "Are you General Hampton?" On his replying that he was, the stranger asked if he remembered capturing and releasing a naked Federal prisoner at a certain time and place in Virginia.

"Yes, I remember it perfectly," answered General Hampton.

"Well," said the stranger, "he is my father. My name is Wade Hampton."

Private Ulysses Robert Brooks,
6th South Carolina Cavalry
Confederate Veteran

Lincoln and the Colonel

I remember the case of the colonel of an eastern regiment who had his wife with him a distance south of Washington, and by an accident his wife was killed. At that time no one was permitted to visit Washington without a permit from the secretary of war.

The colonel obtained the permit and visited Washington, and went to the secretary of war to obtain a permit to take the body of his wife to his home for burial. The secretary refused, and the poor colonel's heart was almost broken. He determined to apply to the president, who was staying at the Soldiers' Home.

He arrived at the Soldiers' Home and saw the president, who seemed disturbed in mind by some adverse news. The colonel made his application, and the president replied, "This is the business of the secretary of war."

"Yes, Mr. President, I have seen the secretary, and he has refused."

The president said, "Sadness is the common heritage of us all, and we must all take our share."

The colonel, with unspeakable sadness, returned to Washington. The next morning, very early, a knock came upon his bedroom door, and there stood the president of the United States. The colonel was amazed. The president said, "Colonel, yesterday I was harsh and unkind to you, and have been unable all night to sleep; come with me."

They went to the secretary of war, obtained the permit, and

the colonel took the body of his dear wife to the hillside of their country home for burial.

That kind and gentle soul could not rest because he thought he had done an unkindness.

Captain Moses Veal,
109th Pennsylvania Infantry
MOLLUS Papers

General Lee's Consideration for His Soldiers

I was a private of Company A, 14th Tennessee Volunteer Infantry, . . . from May 1861, to April 1865. We were marching to Maryland, and as we neared the Potomac River below Winchester, our division—as we understood the entire army was close by— was resting in the shade of a fine body of open timber, through which there was a dim, unused old road. Many of our "boys" were prone upon this road, with knapsacks under our heads, resting, when we noticed the approach of four or five officers on horses.

As they drew near we recognized General A. P. Hill, General Lee, and two or three staff officers. General Hill was a few feet in advance, and, as he drew near to me and others, he said, "Move out of the road, men."

Immediately General Lee said, "Never mind, General; we will ride round them. Lie still, men."

As he spoke he turned his horse to the left, and General Hill was equally as quick to pull out of the road. They passed within twenty feet of me. Did I see General Hill's face flush, or did I imagine it? I do not think General Lee thought of rebuking General Hill, then or ever. It was just his way, his consideration for others, especially his soldiers. . . .

> Private Theodore Hartman,
> 14th Tennessee Infantry
> *Confederate Veteran*

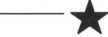

A Masonic Incident

During the Civil War perhaps the strongest fraternal tie binding men together was that of Freemasonry, a bond of fellowship that has been recognized and proved the wide world over as a blessing to mankind.

There were numerous instances in which the sacred tie of Masonry intervened at critical moments, not only in battle, but also in prison pens, where perhaps its luster showed with more brilliance than that radiated by any diamond. Property was preserved, lives protected, and executions stayed by the discovery that the persons involved belonged to the mystic circle, and escaping prisoners of war on both sides, when all hope seemed lost, were succored through its benign influences.

I do not know that I can more forcibly illustrate the truth of this statement than by relating a thrilling incident on the day following the sanguinary battle of Antietam, when a grievously wounded Confederate, who had lain helplessly upon the blood-stained field during the night, with a feeble voice called a member of the 5th New Hampshire Regiment, commanded by that sterling patriot, Colonel Edward E. Cross, who was doing picket duty not far from the Confederate lines, and gave him a slip of soiled paper on which had been marked in a circle, apparently with great effort, some mystic signs. In lieu of a pen or pencil a bit of stick had been used, and his life's blood had been substituted for ink.

"My good fellow," said the wounded and apparently dying Confederate officer, "do me the last earthly favor of handing this piece of paper to some one of your officers whom you may know to be a Freemason. I am dying and would like to give my last message to my family through the medium of one of my brethren."

The New Hampshire soldier, whose heart was full of sympathy for the unfortunate Southron, after covering him with his blanket, making him as comfortable as possible, took the strange-looking missive and, making his dangerous way to the rear, delivered it into the hands of Colonel Cross, who, although a member of the fraternity, was unable to decipher the token so singularly inscribed. The colonel, however, feeling it to be a case of life or death, the bearer of the strange missive having told of the desperate condition of its sender, consulted with Captain J. P. Perry, of his regiment, a member of the thirty-second degree in Masonry, and he had no sooner exhibited to him the missive than the latter somewhat excitedly said, "The man who sent this is a brother Mason in imminent peril and must be rescued."

Colonel Cross . . . at once sent for several brother Masons in his command and, after reciting the strange story, gave them permission to make their way to the perilous spot where the wounded Confederate was seen by the Union soldier and rescue him from a cruel fate. Owing to the close proximity of the two lines of battle and the constant firing of small arms and artillery which prostrated the standing corn as if done by sickles, the relieving party was compelled to crawl upon the ground to the spot where a young and handsome Confederate was found lying in the agonies of death. He had been shot through the thigh and breast and, weak from the loss of blood, was in a state of unconsciousness.

Despite the terrific storm of shot and shell which swept the corn field, imperiling their lives, the New Hampshire brethren shrank not from the performance of a humane duty, and when a lull in the firing came they tenderly placed the young soldier on a stretcher they had thoughtfully taken along and carried him to the field hospital of their regiment, where every attention was given him. Recovering from his insensibility, but too weak to speak, the Confederate manifested his gratitude to his new-found friends, a short time before deadly enemies, for the great service rendered him by mute expressions of love. Removed to the general hospital at Washington, the Southron speedily recovered from his ghastly wounds, and later on was exchanged and permitted to return south.

Confederate Dead at Antietam

The soldier thus rescued from the jaws of death was Lieutenant Jules A. L'Etondal, who belonged to the 12th Alabama regiment and was a member of a Masonic lodge at Mobile. . . .

Often were the strongest friendships formed on the battlefield; for there, amid carnage and desolating scenes, the true heart opens its floodgates and humanity again asserts itself. The enemy, whom but a short time before one is doing his best to kill, you now endeavor to save. You supply him with water to quench his consuming thirst, with your last morsel of food to sustain his strength, and use sympathizing words to soothe his troubled mind.

All that is human or charitable in your nature now rises to your face and you become consecrated by that spirit of mercy that "blesseth him that gives and him that takes. . . ."

I might tell of many instances of this character that came under my observation during the four years' war to show the love that truehearted men, even though enemies, can bear toward one another.

Lieutenant J. Madison Drake,
9th New Jersey Infantry
Confederate Veteran

Clara Barton on the Battlefield

The Sanitary Commission, together with three or four noble, self-sacrificing women, has furnished everything that could be required. I will tell you of one of these women, a Miss Barton, the daughter of Judge Stephen Barton, of Boston, Massachusetts.

I first met her at the battle of Cedar Mountain, where she appeared in front of the hospital at twelve o'clock at night, with a four-mule team loaded with everything needed, and at a time when we were entirely out of dressings of every kind. She supplied us with everything, and while the shells were bursting in every direction, took her course to the hospital on our right, where she found everything wanting again. After doing everything she could on the field, she returned to Culpeper, where she stayed dealing out shirts to the naked wounded, and preparing soup, and seeing it prepared, in all the hospitals. I thought that night if Heaven ever sent out an angel, she must be one, her assistance was so timely.

Well, we began our retreat up the Rappahannock River. I thought no more of our lady friend, only that she had gone back to Washington. We arrived on the disastrous field of Bull Run, and while the battle was raging the fiercest on Friday, who should drive up in front of our hospital but this same woman, with her mules almost dead, having made forced marches from Washington to the army. She was again a welcome visitor to both the wounded and the surgeons.

Random Acts of Kindness

The battle was over, our wounded removed on Sunday, and we were ordered to Fairfax Station. We had hardly got there before the battle of Chantilly commenced, and soon the wounded began to come in. Here we had nothing but our instruments—not even a bottle of wine. When the cars whistled up to the station, the first person on the platform was Miss Barton, to again supply us with bandages, brandy, wine, prepared soup, jellies, meal, and every article that could be thought of. She stayed here until the last wounded soldier was placed on the cars, and then bade us good-bye and left.

I wrote you at the time how we got to Alexandria that night and next morning. Our soldiers had no time to rest after reaching Washington, but were ordered to Maryland by forced marches. Several days of hard marching brought us to Frederick, and the battle of South Mountain followed. The next day our army stood face to face with the whole force. The rattle of 150,000 muskets, and the fearful thunder of over 200 cannon, told us that the great battle of Antietam had commenced. I was in a hospital in the afternoon, for it was then only that the wounded began to come in.

We had expended every bandage, torn up every sheet in the house, and everything we could find, when who should drive up but our old friend Miss Barton, with a team loaded down with dressings of every kind, and everything we could ask for. She distributed her articles to the different hospitals, worked all night making soup, all the next day and night; and when I left, four days after the battle, I left her there ministering to the wounded and the dying. When I returned to the field hospital last week, she was still at work, supplying them with delicacies of every kind, and administering to their wants—all of which she does out of her own private fortune. Now, what do you think of Miss Barton? In my feeble estimation, General McClellan, with all his laurels, sinks into insignificance beside the true heroine of the age—the angel of the battlefield.

Surgeon James L. Dunn
109th Pennsylvania Infantry
Quoted in Moore's *The Civil War in Song and Story*

A Little Girl's Kindness to the Soldiers

After the battle of Sharpsburg, we passed over a line of railroad in central Georgia. The disabled soldiers from General Lee's armies were returning to their homes. At every station the wives and daughters of the farmers came on the cars and distributed food and wines and bandages among the sick and wounded.

We shall never forget how very like an angel was a little girl;—how blushingly and modestly she went to a great rude, bearded soldier, who had carved a crutch from a rough plank to replace a lost leg; how this little girl asked him if he was hungry,—and how he ate like a famished wolf! She asked if his wound was painful, and in a voice of soft, mellow accents, "Can I do nothing more for you? I am sorry that you are so badly hurt; have you a little daughter, and won't she cry when she sees you?"

The rude soldier's heart was touched, and tears of love and gratitude filled his eyes. He only answered, "I have three little children. God grant they may be such angels as you."

With an evident effort he repressed a desire to kiss the fair brow of the pretty little girl. He took her little hand between both his own and bade her "good-bye,—God bless you!" The child will always be a better woman because of these lessons of practical charity stamped ineffaceably upon her young heart.

A Southern newspaper,
Quoted in Moore's *The Civil War in Song and Story*

Homecoming for a Confederate

Several weeks after the battle of Antietam, when our headquarters were at Bunker Hill, I went to Shepherdstown, Virginia, to hear something, if possible, from home. My father lived on the Maryland side of the Potomac, on the crest of a hill, which overlooked the river, the town, and the country beyond. The Potomac was the dividing line between the two states and the two armies, and the bridge that once spanned it there had been burned early in the war.

It was a bright and quiet day, and from the Virginia cliffs I saw the enemy's pickets lying lazily along the canal towpath or wandering over the fields. Up against the hill I saw rifle-pits in a field in front of my home, and bluecoats evidently in possession of it; and then I saw my father come out of the house and walk off toward the barn. I saw no one else except soldiers. It was not a cheerful sight, and I turned away and down to the river to water my horse.

As I rode into the stream several cavalrymen rode in on the other side; they saluted me by lifting their hats and I returned their salute. They invited me, laughingly, to come over, and I, being intensely anxious to hear something from home, replied that I would meet them in the middle of the river. They at once drew out of the water and dismounted, and so did I and the courier who was with me. Half a dozen of them got into the ferryboat, which was on their side, and we embarked in a leaky skiff, my courier using a paddle which he found at hand. We met the enemy's man-of-war in the middle of the stream and grappled it, while it was held in place with poles by its boatmen.

After the first greetings, the captain of the gunboat (he was only a sergeant, by the way) said to me, "I see you are a staff officer."

My blunt courier broke in gruffly, "Yes, and don't you think it devilish hard for a man to be this near home and not be able to speak to his father or mother?"

This exposure of my identity was the very thing I did not wish. The sergeant looked a little astonished and replied, "So you are Captain Douglas, of General Jackson's staff, are you? We knew that the old gentleman on the hill has two sons in the Confederate army, one on the general's staff."

When I acknowledged his correctness, he said, with much earnestness, that I must get into their boat and go over to see my family. I began to protest that it would not do, when one of the others broke in, "Say, get in, Captain, get in. If this government can be busted up by a Rebel soldier going to see his mother, why, damn it, let it bust!"

There was a laughing chorus of assent to this that shook my doubts. I told my blue-coated friends that there was no officer among them, and that any officer who caught me on the other side might not recognize their safeguard and I might be detained. The sergeant replied that all their officers were in Sharpsburg at a dinner, and at any rate, this party would pledge themselves to return me safely. It was an occasion for some risk and I took it. I got into the large boat and my courier came along in his skiff "to see fair play," as he grimly said.

When we reached the Maryland shore, the soldiers on the bank crowded down to the boats, and soon, Yankee-like, were in a full tide of questions, especially about Stonewall Jackson. As I had declined to leave our ships for the purpose of going up to my home, a cavalryman had gone to the house, under spur, to notify my family of my arrival. My mother soon made her appearance, very much frightened, for she believed I could only be there as a prisoner. My father, not being allowed to leave his premises without permission, could not come. As my mother approached, the soldiers, at a signal from the sergeant, drew away and sat down on the towpath, where they and my courier interviewed each other.

As this strange meeting gave my mother more anxiety than comfort, it was a brief one. Nothing passed between us, however, that could "bust the government" or bring trouble on the sergeant and his men. When my mother left and took her stand upon the canal bank to see us safely off, the soldiers gathered about me to have a little talk, but I did not tarry. I gave the sergeant and his crew of the man-of-war my autograph upon sundry slips of paper, and told them that if the fortune of war should make them prisoners, the little papers might be of service to them if sent to General Jackson's headquarters.

As we took our leave and got into our skiff, the chivalric, manly sergeant said to me, "We belong to"—I think —"The 1st New York Cavalry. My parents live on the banks of the Hudson, and what I have done for you, I'd like someone to do for me if in the same fix. While I'm here I'll keep an eye on your home and people and do what I can for them" (and he did). And as the skiff moved over the water and took me from home again, I raised my hat to my "good friend, the enemy," and they stood along the shore, in response, with uncovered heads; and then I waved it to my father, who stood on the stone wall which crowns the hill and gazed, but made no sign; and then to my mother on the bank, who, seeing me safely off, waved her handkerchief with a tremulous flutter, and then hid her face in it as she turned and hurried away.

Major Henry Kyd Douglas,
General Thomas J. Jackson's staff
Quoted by *History of the Corn Exchange Regiment*

Arkansas Soldiers in Virginia

The 3rd Arkansas Regiment of Infantry was the sole representative of our state in the Army of Northern Virginia for nearly two years. We were brigaded with the 30th Virginia (from Fredericksburg and vicinity) and the 27th and 46th North Carolina. The Virginia and Arkansas soldiers became better acquainted and more intimate than the other regiments; indeed, we became very social and friendly.

Shortly after the awful fatigues and marches of the first Maryland campaign, culminating in the bloody battle of Sharpsburg, the troops were camped somewhere between Shepherdstown and Winchester. We were sorely in need of clothing and shoes, and there was not a blanket in the command, while the frosty nights of that cold climate pinched severely.

At that time the 30th Virginia received a considerable supply of shoes and blankets from their friends and relatives at Fredericksburg, about eighty miles distant. When these supplies arrived, we of the 3rd Arkansas were surprised to receive a message from the headquarters of the 30th, requesting that we send a detail to receive our share of these good things. Colonel Van H. Manning called a meeting of the officers, and we passed some resolutions warmly thanking the Virginians for their generous offer, but declining to accept on the ground that the donors of those goods intended them for the relief of their own kin.

The reply came back immediately and in the strongest terms, "We are brothers fighting in the same cause, and, besides, you are a long distance from home, and it is impossible for your friends to help you. We insist upon it that we divide." And they did.

Some months afterwards we had an opportunity to show our appreciation of this kind and generous act. The great battle of Fredericksburg was fought. One hundred and fifty pieces of heavy artillery planted on Stafford Heights poured shot and shell upon the old town. The women and children had to crawl into the cellars, while their houses were being battered down over their heads; and not only this, but while the enemy occupied the town they robbed the citizens of everything they could lay their hands on.

After we had driven the enemy back across the river and the town had been evacuated, word came to us that there were a number of women and children actually starving. The 3rd Arkansas immediately took the initiative. We divided our rations in half (and they were slim enough, God knows) and stirred among the other regiments and gathered quite a little supply of food which we sent over, relieving their immediate necessities. Sometime afterwards the ladies of Fredericksburg sent us a beautiful new silk flag.

I know not what others may think, but in my judgment this incident deserves to be recorded in Confederate history, as do the most heroic deeds of personal valor.

Captain Alexander C. Jones,
3rd Arkansas Infantry
Confederate Veteran

When Duty Demanded Disobedience

The sensibilities of Lieutenant Lemuel L. Crocker had been aroused by the necessary abandonment of the dead and wounded, left uncared for and unattended in the precipitate withdrawal after the battle of Shepherdstown, Virginia, on October 1, 1862. He entreated Colonel James Barnes so earnestly for permission to go and care for the forsaken ones, that the colonel, fully comprehending the impropriety of the request, at last reluctantly consented to present it to General Fitz-John Porter, the corps commander. It met with a flat, emphatic refusal. There was no communication with the enemy, and it was not proposed to open any. War was war, and this was neither the time nor the occasion for sentiment or sympathy.

But Crocker was not to be deterred in his errand of mercy, and, in positive disregard of instructions, proceeded deliberately, fully accoutered with sword, belt and pistol, to cross the Potomac River at the breast of the dam. It was a novel spectacle for an officer, armed with all he was entitled to carry, to thus commence a lonesome advance against a whole army corps. Bound upon an unauthorized mission of peace and humanity, a little experience might have taught him his reception would have been more cordial if he had left his weapons at home. Still, it was Crocker's heart at work, and its honest, manly beats bade him face the danger.

He found the bodies of Saunders, Ricketts, and Moss, and Private Mishaw badly wounded, but still alive. He was bearing them, one by one, upon his shoulders to the riverbank, when he was suddenly interrupted by an orderly from General Porter, who informed him that he was instructed to direct him to return at once or he would order a battery to shell him out. His reply was, "Shell and be damned!" He didn't propose to return until the full purpose of his undertaking had been accomplished.

The orderly thus abruptly disposed of, he continued his operations, when he was again interrupted by an authority which, if it failed to command respect, could enforce obedience. He had carried all the bodies to the bank, and was returning for the wounded Mishaw, when a Confederate general— whom Crocker always thought was Lee, but in this he was evidently mistaken— accompanied by a numerous staff, came upon the ground. An aide-de-camp rode up, inquiring, with some asperity— explaining that no flag of truce was in operation—as to who and what he was, his purpose of being there, and by whose authority.

Lieutenant Lemuel L. Crocker

Crocker's work, which he had conducted wholly himself, had put him in a sorry plight. He was of large frame, muscular, and finely proportioned. He had carried the bodies over his left shoulder and was absolutely covered with blood and dirt, almost unrecognizable as a soldier, and his voice and form alone indicated his manhood.

His reply was prompt and ingenuous: he had been refused permission to cross by his corps commander, to whom he had made his purpose known; the dead and wounded of the regiment that fought on that ground yesterday were of the blood of Philadelphia's best citizens, and, regardless of the laws of war and the commands of his superiors, he was of the opinion that humanity and decency demanded that they be properly cared for, which, no one else attempting, he had determined to risk the consequences and discharge the duty himself.

The simplicity and earnestness of this reply prompted the further interrogation as to how long he had been in the service.

"Twenty days," responded Crocker.

The gentle, "I thought so" from the lips of the veteran general showed that the ingenuousness and sincerity had wholly captured him. He bade him continue his labors until they were fully completed, pointed out a boat on the shore that he could utilize to ferry his precious freight across the stream, and surrounded the field with a cordon of cavalry patrols to protect him from further molestation or interruption.

But Crocker had a host of troubles to face upon his return. He had openly violated the positive commands of his superior; he had been shamefully insulting to the messenger who bore his superior's instructions, and had acted in utter disregard of well-known laws governing armies confronting each other. Still, there was something about the whole affair, so honest, so earnest, and so true, that there was a disposition to temporize with the stern demands of discipline. And he had fully accomplished his purpose—all the bodies and the wounded man were safely landed on the Maryland side. However, he was promptly arrested.

Colonel Barnes, who had watched him through all his operations, was the first of his superiors who was prompted to leniency, and he accompanied him to corps headquarters to intercede in his behalf. They were ushered into the presence of General Porter, who, shocked at such a wholesale accumulation of improprieties, and angered to a high tension by such positive disobediences, proceeded, in short and telling phrases, to explain the law and regulations—all of which, if Crocker didn't know before he started, he had had full opportunity to gather in during his experiences.

Then followed moments of painful silence, and the general inquired whether he had seen a gun the regulars had left upon the other side the day before, and if so, what was the likelihood of its recovery. Crocker replied that he had not, but had noticed a caisson, and that he did not consider it likely it would ever come back. Returning to the subject, the general continued his reproof; but, considering his inexperience, unquestioned courage, and evident good intentions, he finally yielded, concluding that the reprimand was sufficient punishment, and released him from arrest and restored him to duty.

History of the Corn Exchange Regiment

Greater Love Hath No Man

This is the story of Hiram Smith, a Missourian, who laid down his life for a friend. Over his grave in a little country cemetery there stands a granite monument which the friend's son bought with money he saved the first winter he taught school. He could not pay the debt his family owed this humble dead man, but he could show that he remembered. It happened this way:

When General John McNeil, Federal commander, made his headquarters in Palmyra, Missouri, in 1862, he found two counties, Marion and Lewis, torn by guerrilla warfare of a bloody sort. McNeil placed in jail a number of the most influential Confederate sympathizers within reach and held them as hostages for good behavior. What happened to them would depend upon how their friends restrained themselves. One of the men in jail was William T. Humphrey, a farmer and the father of seven children.

Now, the jail at Palmyra was crowded, and soon some of the prisoners were paroled. Among them was Humphrey. He and two of his neighbors signed a bond, pledging their farms that he would keep his parole. He was not to go beyond the limits of the town site of Palmyra. Then the jail burned, so that all the prisoners had to be released, and Humphrey was told that he might go home, but must report at Federal headquarters at regular intervals.

And then an ominous thing happened in Marion County. A farmer, a strong Union man, disappeared. It was believed that he had been slain by Southern sympathizers, and there has never been anything to disprove the theory. No trace of the man or the man's body was ever found. And the men who knew did not talk.

McNeil posted an order throughout the countryside. If the man was not produced alive or his murderers brought in to headquarters within five days, ten Confederate sympathizers would be shot. The chances are that General McNeil never imagined that he would be called upon to carry out his threat. But when three days had passed in vain, he gave orders to William R. Strachan, his provost marshal, to collect ten men.

That day William Humphrey came into Palmyra to report on his parole and promptly was shut up in the basement of the building that was Federal headquarters. There were other men with him, good friends; William Baker, of Lewis County, was one, and Thomas A. Sidner another. They, too, must die.

That night there was furious riding in the country around Palmyra, and in the dawn there was hitching of teams, and grave men and haggard women came into the town. Was this thing true? They must at least see their friends.

From William Humphrey's farm there came a wagon carrying his wife and seven little children. And Mrs. Humphrey (and the seven were with her) saw General McNeil. She pleaded for her husband's life. Surely he had dealt honorably with his enemies. Had he ever failed to keep his parole? He had not. They were young, the seven, to be left with no provider.

McNeil was not untouched. There was justice in this mother's plea. Her husband had kept his promises. He called Humphrey into the room and told him to stay there while he tried to find a substitute. And he sent out his provost marshal on that errand.

The prisoners had many visitors that day. William Baker's son-in-law, Hiram Smith, had come in from a little far-off farm among the brakes, where he and his wife lived. They were poor people and tenants. They had no children. Hiram Smith was in the yard outside, preparing to go home, when the provost marshal approached him.

"What is your name?" asked Strachan.

"Hiram Smith," the young farmer replied.

"I have a warrant for you," said the provost marshal and wrote Smith's name into a blank death warrant.

Smith said nothing. He looked up at the open window where William Humphrey stood, his wife and children with him. Hiram Smith raised his eyebrows in question. "Are you the man to be saved?" his glance asked. Humphrey nodded. Can you imagine the dumbness that was on the man and how tight his throat must have been as he nodded?

And Smith turned simply to the provost marshal. "It had better be me than that man with such a family," he said quietly.

They walked across a little courtyard to the prison place. There was a well, and Hiram Smith stopped for a drink of water. "The way it is," he said to the marshal, "I can die as easily as drink that water." And he went inside the building.

William Humphrey did not go home that night, though. It seemed that Hiram Smith did not know how to write. There were some letters he would like to leave. So through the night the two men were together. Smith told Humphrey what he would like to say, and Humphrey wrote it down. He thought of his wife and the seven children, and he thought of this young man who could die so quietly. And the night passed.

McNeil delayed all morning. He hoped that at the last the slayers might come in and save the ten. They did not come.

There had been ten board coffins built, and when afternoon came the men and the coffins were taken out into a public place, and each man was ordered to sit on the end of his coffin.

There were three men with rifles for each of the condemned. And their friends and their relatives, whoever would, might see the execution of the sentence. It should be a lesson. McNeil's men were good shots. They did not bungle the job.

Hiram Smith's body was buried in a little neighborhood graveyard. For a long time, only a white board that grew more weatherworn from year to year marked his grave. But the Humphreys did not forget the humble grave, and it was George W. Humphrey, born two years after Hiram Smith's death, who spent the savings of his first winter of school teaching to build a monument over the man who died to save his father. . . .

Confederate Veteran

Buck's Baby

Buck Denman, . . . a Mississippi bear hunter and a superb specimen of manhood, was color sergeant of the 21st Mississippi and a member of Captain Lane W. Brandon's company. He was tall and straight, broad-shouldered and deep-chested, had an eye like an eagle and a voice like a bull of Bashan, and was as full of pluck and power as a panther. He was as rough as a bear in manner, but withal a noble, tenderhearted fellow, and a splendid soldier.

During the skirmishing and fierce shelling that preceded the battle of Fredericksburg, Buck's regiment was ordered to fall back. The enemy, finding the way now clear, were coming up the street, full company front, with flags flying and bands playing, while the great shells from the siege guns were bursting over their heads and dashing their hurtling fragments after our retreating skirmishers.

Buck was behind the corner of a house taking sight for a last shot. Just as his finger trembled on the trigger,

Skirmishing at Fredericksburg

a little three-year-old, fair-haired, baby girl toddled out of an alley, accompanied by a Newfoundland dog, and gave chase to a big shell that was rolling lazily along the pavement, she clapping her little hands and the dog snapping and barking furiously at the shell.

Buck's hand dropped from the trigger. He dashed it across his eyes to dispel the mist and make sure he hadn't passed over the river and wasn't seeing his own baby girl in a vision. No, there is the baby, amid the hell of shot and shell, and here come the enemy. A moment and he has grounded his gun, dashed out into the storm, swept his great right arm around the baby, gained cover again, and, baby clasped to his breast and musket trailed in his left hand, is trotting after the boys up to Marye's Heights.

And there behind that historic stone wall, and in the lines hard by, all those hours and days of terror was that baby kept, her fierce nurses taking turns patting her, while the storm of battle raged and shrieked, and at night wrestling with each other for the boon and benediction of her quiet breathing under their blankets. Never was a baby so cared for. They scoured the countryside for milk, and conjured up their best skill to prepare dainty viands for her little ladyship.

When the struggle was over and the enemy had withdrawn to his strongholds across the river, and General William Barksdale was ordered to reoccupy the town, the 21st Mississippi, having held the post of danger in the rear, was given the place of honor in the van and led the column. There was a long halt, the brigade and regimental staff hurrying to and fro. The regimental colors could not be found.

Denman stood about the middle of the regiment, baby in arms. Suddenly he sprang to the front. Swinging her aloft above his head, her little garments fluttering like the folds of a banner, he shouted, "Forward, 21st, here are your colors!" and without further order, off started the brigade toward the town, yelling as only Barksdale's men could yell. They were passing through a street fearfully shattered by the enemy's fire and were shouting their very souls out, but let Buck himself describe the last scene in the drama:

"I was holding the baby high . . . , with both arms, when above all the racket I heard a woman's scream. The next thing I knew I was covered with calico, and she fainted on my breast. I caught her before she fell, and laying her down gently, put the baby on her bosom. She was most the prettiest thing I ever looked at, and her eyes were shut;—and—I hope God'll forgive me, but I kissed her just once."

Private Robert Stiles,
First Company, Richmond Howitzers
Four Years Under Marse Robert

The Angel of Marye's Heights

Richard Kirkland was the son of John Kirkland, an estimable citizen of Kershaw County, South Carolina, a plain, substantial farmer of the olden time. In 1861 he entered as a private in Captain J.D. Kennedy's Company E of the 2nd South Carolina Volunteers, in which company he was a sergeant in December 1862.

The day after the sanguinary battle of Fredericksburg, General Joseph B. Kershaw's brigade occupied the road at the foot of Marye's Hill and the ground about Marye's house, the scene of their desperate defense of the day before. One hundred and fifty yards in front of the road, the stone facing of which constituted the famous stone wall, lay General George Sykes' division of regulars, U.S.A., between whom and our troops a murderous skirmish occupied the whole day, fatal to many who heedlessly exposed themselves, even for a moment. The ground between the lines was bridged with the wounded, dead, and dying Federals, victims of the many desperately gallant assaults of that column of 30,000 brave men hurled vainly against that impregnable position.

All that day those wounded men rent the air with their groans and their agonizing cries of "Water! Water!" In the afternoon, General Kershaw sat in the north room, upstairs, of Mrs. Stevens' house, in front of the road, surveying the field, when Kirkland came up. With an expression of indignant remonstrance pervading his person, his manner, and the tone of his voice, he said, "General! I can't stand this."

"What is the matter, Sergeant?" asked the general.

He replied, "All night and all day I have heard those poor people crying for water, and I can stand it no longer. I come to ask permission to go and give them water."

The general regarded him for a moment with feelings of profound admiration and said, "Kirkland, don't you know that you would get a bullet through your head the moment you stepped over the wall?"

"Yes, sir," he said, "I know that; but if you will let me, I am willing to try it."

After a pause, the general said, "Kirkland, I ought not to allow you to run such a risk, but the sentiment which actuates you is so noble that I will not refuse your request, trusting that God may protect you. You may go."

The sergeant's eye lighted up with pleasure. He said, "Thank you, sir," and ran rapidly downstairs. The general heard him pause for a moment, and then return, bounding two steps at a time. He thought the sergeant's heart had failed him. He was mistaken. The sergeant stopped at the door and said, "General, can I show a white handkerchief?"

The general slowly shook his head, saying emphatically, "No, Kirkland, you can't do that."

"All right," he said, "I'll take the chances," and ran down with a bright smile on his handsome countenance.

With profound anxiety he was watched as he stepped over the wall on his errand of mercy—Christ-like mercy. Unharmed, he reached the nearest sufferer. He knelt beside him, tenderly raised the drooping head, rested it gently upon his own noble breast, and poured the precious life-giving fluid down the fever-scorched throat. This done, he laid him tenderly down, placed his knapsack under his head, straightened out his broken limb, spread his overcoat over him, replaced his empty canteen with a full one, and turned to another sufferer.

By this time his purpose was well understood on both sides, and all danger was over. From all parts of the field arose fresh cries of "Water, water; for God's sake, water!" More piteous still, the mute appeal of some who could only feebly lift a hand to say here, too, is life and suffering.

For an hour and a half did this ministering angel pursue his labor of mercy, nor ceased to go and return until he relieved all the wounded on that part of the field. He returned to his post wholly unhurt. Who shall say how sweet his rest that winter's night beneath the cold stars!

Sergeant Richard R. Kirkland

Little remains to be told. Sergeant Kirkland distinguished himself in battle at Gettysburg and was promoted to lieutenant. At Chickamauga he fell on the field of battle, in the hour of victory. He was but a youth when called away and had never formed those ties from which might have resulted a posterity to enjoy his fame and bless his country; but he had bequeathed to the American youth—yea, to the world— an example which dignifies our common humanity.

Brigadier General Joseph B. Kershaw
Charleston New and Courier

A Confederate Christmas

After the Confederate army—or "our army," as we used to say—fell back from Manassas in the spring of 1862, we were in the enemy's country. My home was in the little village of Warrenton, just in the track of both armies. In the morning the Yankees would have possession, and maybe that afternoon "our men" would be marching through. But this winter the Yankees had gone into winter quarters, and the people of the little village had settled down to make the best of it.

Now, it is very hard for the people of the South to think of a good Yankee. We know of all the horrors of the latter years of this cruel war; but a gentleman is always the same wherever he is born, and there were a great many kind Yankees, and that winter many kind things were done by these men who, although our enemies, were living among us.

Well, I have made a long preface to a short story. As I said, the troops had gone into winter quarters; no more dashing in of "our men" to cheer us up by telling of how things were going on "across the lines," and we children looked forward to a dull Christmas. To give us a little pleasure, Mrs. General P., whose husband was in Richmond, formed a dancing class, and twice a week we would meet in her parlors and she would play on the piano for us to dance. There were about eight girls and as many boys. The old-fashioned lancers, the quadrilles, and the waltzes were learned.

When Christmas came, we wanted to send a little Christmas present to Mrs. P., to show how we appreciated the pleasure she had given us, but what could we do? There were no stores to sell and no money to buy. The Yankees had their sutlers, who were sometimes allowed to sell to the citizens; but they were not then allowed to do so, for it had been reported that we bought provisions to save up for the "Rebels."

You will recall what I have just said, that "we had no money;" but when the Yankees came to stay, they used to buy homemade bread, and would furnish materials for the ladies to make pies and cakes, and our mothers were willing to do anything to get some Yankee money, or "greenbacks," as we called the paper money. So each of us determined to get a little money from our parents. We collected three dollars, which was a "whole heap" for us, but how were we to spend it? Recess each day found us consulting on this important question. It was at last decided that we would buy some sugar and tea and coffee, but where were we to get it?

Again came the consultation, when one of the girls, Lillie P., said, "Why, there is a very nice Yankee who has his headquarters in the lot next to our house, and I believe he would let us buy it if we asked him."

Then came the question, "Who is going to face the enemy?" We determined that five of the girls should go, so Mollie S., Florie T., Jennie P., myself, and sister were chosen. The girl who proposed it was to introduce us.

You can hardly imagine a more scared set of little girls; but we must get our present, so down we marched and asked the sentinel who walked in front of the officers' tent if we could see Colonel Gardener (I remember the name and wish I could remember the regiment) on "important business." In a few minutes we were ushered into his presence. I was to be the spokesman, but I am sure if the colonel had not been so gentle and kind my mouth would never have been able to open.

Well, after a fashion, we made known our errand and offered our pitiful little three dollars, which meant so much to us, asking if he would let his sutler sell us that amount in sugar and coffee. Why, certainly, it should be sent to us that afternoon. You can hardly think how glad we were and how we thanked the Yankee colonel.

Now the pleasant part of my story comes. That afternoon up came the colonel's orderly with twenty pounds of sugar and a large package of coffee and tea (I suppose five times as much as our money would have bought) and a nice letter with three one-dollar greenbacks, saying that he was glad to contribute to the brave little girls who wished to give a Christmas present to the wife of a Confederate general who had given her time for their amusement.

Our delight can hardly be described to the little ones of today who have all they want for their comfort and amusement, and I believe that everybody who takes the trouble to read this little story will be glad to know that even in those hard days there were kind Yankees who did feel sorry for the little Confederate girls; and it is just as nice, as the years go by, to remember these kind acts, while it does good also to tell them. And always remember that the old-fashioned name of gentleman or gentlewoman belongs to the person who so behaves, and not to any locality or country.

Janet H. Weaver Randolph
Confederate Veteran

Kindness of General Jeff C. Davis

In the battle of Murfreesboro, December 31, 1862, we charged the right flank of the enemy. We surprised and routed their first line, driving it in wild confusion for some miles, when suddenly we encountered a new line secreted in a cedar glade. At this point, I saw General James E. Rains fall from his horse, mortally wounded and, as I turned to tell one of my men that General Rains had fallen, a minie ball penetrated three of my ribs and paralyzed my right leg.

I was carried to the field hospital and from there to the residence of Mr. B. W. Henry, where I remained undisturbed for about three weeks, receiving the best of care and attention. My wound was healing nicely, though I was still confined to my bed when a Federal officer with six guards came into my room and said he had orders from General Jeff C. Davis to take me to his headquarters.

After walking a mile and a half I was halted in front of General Davis' headquarters and left alone. When the general saw me, he advanced toward me, saying, "Who are you."

"My name is McCauley."

"What are you, and who brought you here?"

"I am a captain in the Confederate army." I was offering an explanation when I saw the officer who had conveyed me there, and pointed him out to the general.

The general called the officer to him and asked him about the same questions he had asked me, and then, with a closed fist and pointed finger said, "There are some men that do not seem to have a damn bit of sense. I told you to go out into the country and bring in our men that may be straggling out from camp."

The general then took me by the arm, asked me into his marquee, and told me to lie down on his cot. I thanked him, but declined his offer, and when he asked why, I told him that my wound was bleeding. He then placed a campstool near me and asked me to sit down, which I did with thanks, as I was feeling very weak and sick. The staff seemed to be busy drawing up reports and maps of the battle.

The general asked me whose brigade I was in and on what part of the line. I told him, and added that we surprised and routed one line of his men, and pursued them about one and a half miles, then encountered a second line posted in a cedar glade, and found them very stubborn; that at this place General Rains was killed and I was wounded.

The general's face indicated much interest, and he said, "I placed the line in the cedars and know the very spot on which General Rains fell."

I gave him all the information I could relative to the positions occupied by the opposing armies, and asked him to assign me to some place to spend the night, as I was very weak and sick. He asked me where I wanted to go, and I mentioned Mr. Henry's.

He gave me a note written by himself saying, "I will send you to the provost marshal and he will send you where you want to go."

He directed a courier to get an ambulance but I told him I did not want to ride, as the jarring would tear my wound, and he said that he had a good, old gentle horse. I thanked him and accepted the horse. On account of the wound in my leg, I had difficulty in mounting, seeing which the general took hold of my leg, lifted it gently over the saddle, stepped round to the other side of the horse, placed my foot in the stirrup and asked how I felt. He then gave me his hand with a fond "good-bye."

We soon reached the provost marshal's office. That officer, after requiring me to sign a parole of honor, ordered the courier to conduct me to Mr. Henry's home. . . .

Captain William H. McCauley,
11th Tennessee Infantry
Confederate Veteran

1863

TRIALS AND TRIUMPHS

Random Acts of Kindness

Going Home

Among the prisoners captured by our troops in the late battle of Fredericksburg was a wounded Rebel officer, Captain Edward P. Lawton, a brother of General Alexander R. Lawton. He received at the hands of our soldiers and surgeons the same treatment as our own wounded, and with them was sent to the hospital at Alexandria, Virginia.

A few days since, a flag of truce brought the captain's wife into our lines, who was kindly received by General Edwin V. Sumner, commanding the right wing of our army here, and by him sent to rejoin her husband. On her arrival at Alexandria, she found but her husband's corpse, he having some time previously died of his wounds.

In her grief and anxiety to pay the last tribute of love and respect to his remains, she sought and obtained permission to convey them to her home in Georgia for interment, and yesterday arrived at the Falmouth railroad station with the body encased in a metallic coffin. There, Lieutenant Colonel W. W. Teall of General Sumner's staff courteously took the sorrowful lady and her charge under his care, and prepared for their transportation under a flag of truce to the opposite side of the Rappahannock River. The coffin having been transferred to an ambulance, an escort was provided from the 10th New York (National Zouaves), who now form the bodyguard of General Sumner, and placed under the command of Lieutenant George F. Tait, of that regiment. With muffled drum and arms reversed, the cortege—mournful, yet retaining something of cheerfulness in their bright-colored and picturesque uniforms—wound their way from Sumner's head-quarters to the bank of the Rappahannock.

Notice having previously been sent, a large party had gathered on the farther side, in expectation of the remains, and a procession was already formed to receive them. The Union party and their Southern charge having crossed the river, the lady returned her heartfelt thanks to Lieutenant Colonel Teall.

The Rebel general Kershaw, to whose care she was consigned, spoke feelingly of the magnanimity shown forth in these marks of respect to a fallen foe; of his surprise and gratification at witnessing them, and promised never to forget the honor awarded by a generous enemy to a departed comrade. May this feeling extend to all now in arms against the country that gave them birth—that nursed and protected them—and which they are now seeking to divide and destroy.

But the strangest scene which the south bank of the Rappahannock yesterday presented was the mingling in friendly conversation of men who but a few short weeks ago stood opposed in deadly conflict, pouring a hail of lead into each other's breasts, and animated by all the hate and fury which such a strife must engender—men, too, who may at any moment be called on to repeat, act by act, the late bloody drama behind Fredericksburg. Yet white-turbaned and blue-jacketed Zouave conversed seriously or cracked his wild joke, despite the occasion, with gray-coated Rebel, and officers amicably discussed battles wherein they had strained every nerve to accomplish each other's destruction. But at length the strangely assorted party separated, the Rebels returning to their batteries, our men to their encampments, both to await a meeting of a different kind from this.

New York Herald,
Quoted by *Mobile Advertiser and Register*

Modesty Becomes Her

Mosby . . . was wounded at Murfreesboro, Tennessee, captured, and taken to Nashville, where with many others he was put in the penitentiary, then used as a Federal prison. Among the prisoners was a Confederate who had lost all his clothing except his under-garments; and, as it was rumored that all of the prisoners would soon be sent North, he was much troubled over his dilemma.

One day, a young lady of Nashville visiting the prison either saw or heard of this young soldier's condition, and, leaving, she returned in a short time. She told the prisoners to turn their backs, and taking off a pair of trousers she had smuggled in under her dress, she said, "Give these pants to that young man, and tell him to wear them as I did to get them in here." The young lady may yet be living; if so, she will be glad to know that her kindly deed has been remembered all these years.

Sergeant William A. Campbell,
11th Mississippi Cavalry
Confederate Veteran

Mrs. Sarah Bell Waller

During the late Civil War, Mrs. Waller was one of the most untiring, persevering, and efficient friends of the Confederate prisoners of war, confined at Camp Douglas, near Chicago. Every few days, accompanied by her little daughter, Bell, she visited the camp with clothing for the needy and hospital supplies for the sick. This she continued as long as Camp Douglas was occupied as a prison pen for captured Confederates, which was until the war closed.

Her work was done in a thoroughly honorable and business-like way, acting always under the express permission and with the full knowledge and approval of the Federal officer in command of the prison. A strict account was kept of all her receipts and disbursements by a mercantile house in this city that assisted her in this work. She accompanied every delivery of clothing and supplies for the prisoners, and in person exacted and obtained the receipts of the commissary of prisoners, through whom deliveries were made to the prisoners. Up to the time of the "big fire" in Chicago, in 1871, a complete record of all her receipts and disbursements was in existence, but, unfortunately, these were destroyed at that time. Were they now in existence, a detailed report of her work, showing its magnitude and the difficulties which she encountered and overcame in carrying it out, would not only astonish, but touch the heart and awaken the sincere gratitude of every true Southern man and woman now living.

As it is, memory is the only source of information now attainable. It would make this communication too long to enter fully into the details which even memory can yet supply. A single line of these great services, which is indeed but an item in the lengthy account, is here given to illustrate, though feebly, the magnitude of the work done by this big-hearted Southern woman and those who assisted her, the amount of suffering it relieved, and the many lives saved by it.

The Arkansas Post prisoners were brought to Chicago in mid-winter 1863, numbering, I believe, about three thousand men; all being from the far South, were thinly clad and ill-prepared to withstand the rigors of a Chicago winter, and much suffering from frosted feet and limbs resulted, which was soon followed by lung pneumonia, which became almost an epidemic among them and from which large numbers died. Through Mrs.

Mrs. Sarah Bell Waller

Waller's instrumentality and the generous donations of friends in Kentucky, Maryland, and New York, she had the great satisfaction of seeing them at least comfortably clothed.

There was never a time when money sufficient to buy any one kind of garment for all was on hand, but beginning with heavy, woolen shirts and continuing till all were supplied with these, then drawers, and then shoes and socks. Socks were always in abundance from Kentucky, but to shoe so many men with the means at command, seemed almost an impossibility.

With the permission of the commandant, and his cooperation in supplying the necessary quarters to work in, Mrs. Waller established a shoemaker's shop and found about a dozen shoe-makers among the prisoners who were willing to work. These were supplied with outfits of tools and material for mending old shoes, and between the old shoes repaired and the new shoes she was enabled to furnish, she got them fairly well shod.

Next in order came pants—here was another almost hopeless task, for just about this time orders came from Washington prohibiting prisoners of war from receiving outside clothing from their friends of any other than butternut color. This was not a fashionable color in Chicago and Mrs. Waller almost came to the conclusion that her work was at an end, but "where there's the will there's a way." A piece of an old butternut-colored jeans coat was obtained and with it a piece of blue kersey—with these the dye-house was visited to ascertain if the blue could be converted into butternut. It was a success. Three hundred pair of condemned Federal blue pants were purchased and converted into the desired butternut. I don't think I ever saw a more pleased woman in my life than was Mrs. Waller when starting to Camp Douglas with this first installment of the regulation butternut pants.

Suffice to say that she persevered, one kind of a garment at a time, till she had the extreme satisfaction of seeing these Arkansas Post prisoners at least comfortably clothed. Prisoners from Fort Donelson, Island Number 10, Shiloh, and, in fact, from nearly all the battlefields of Kentucky, Tennessee, and Mississippi, that were quartered at Camp Douglas have especial cause to remember Mrs. Waller with feelings of gratitude.

When the difficulties and drawbacks which attended, surrounded, and hampered this great work from first to last are remembered and fully considered, the close and arbitrary rules of those in authority, the jealousy and bitterness of the surrounding population, the great number of sick and thinly-clothed prisoners brought to Chicago during the war, so much suffering and with such limited means to relieve it, it is especially due the memory of this brave, gifted, whole-souled woman that her work of humanity, to which she devoted four years of her life with untiring industry, should be known by the survivors, descendants, and kindred of those she so earnestly labored for. . . .

W.O.G.
Southern Bivouac

The Good Georgia Governor

A gentleman who left this city last week, to see Governor Joseph E. Brown on some official business, was directed at Canton, the residence of the governor, to proceed to his farm, where he would find him. On his way thither, he overtook and passed a large number of small wagons, carts, etc., with numerous foot passengers, all proceeding to the same destination, and when he arrived there, to his surprise, he saw that quite a large number of men and women, with vehicles of the same description, were around the corncribs and barn of the governor, who was engaged in the distribution to them of corn, shucks, etc., in proportion to the size of their families and their wants.

Upon inquiring, the gentleman learned that those who had gathered there were the poor wives, widows, and children of the soldiers from Cherokee County, among whom Governor Brown was distributing his surplus corn. The sight was a most grateful one to our traveler, who came back to Atlanta impressed with the double conviction of Governor Brown being not only a good governor, but a good man. The grateful tears which he saw in the eyes of the good women of Cherokee, who were being made the recipients of Governor Brown's patriotic liberality, made an impression upon him which, he says, will be lasting, and which has taught him not to be chary in his charities in the future.

Atlanta Daily Intelligencer

Generous Action of a Comrade

During a pause in one of the engagements fought in Virginia, Colonel Matthew C. Butler, of Hampton's cavalry, and Captain W. D. Farley, the famous scout, were sitting quietly on horseback talking together, when suddenly a ball struck Colonel Butler above the ankle, passed through his horse, killing it, proceeded to crush Captain Farley's leg, and killed his horse also.

Some of the soldiers rushed quickly forward and disengaged the fallen officers from their dead horses, but it was found that both of these gentlemen would have to suffer the amputation of a limb. Surgeons were sent for, and they were laid in the shade of a big tree nearby.

When the surgeon, Dr. B. W. Taylor, arrived to perform the double operation, he first approached Colonel Butler, the ranking officer, and said to him, "Colonel, I have very little chloroform, but I will share it equally between you and the Captain."

"No," replied Colonel Butler, "keep it all for Farley, who is worse off than I am. I can bear the pain without it."

The ordeal was accordingly endured, without the aid of this alleviating adjunct of surgery, and the generous hero happily survived the operation!

As soon as he was able to ride, Butler returned to the field of duty, resumed the command of his regiment, and rose to be the youngest (and the handsomest) major general in the service of the Confederate States. . . .

1863

The gallant Farley died a few days after the above-mentioned incident, in spite of the magnanimous self-renunciation of his comrade.

Claudine Rhett
Confederate Veteran

The Episode of Patrick Conley

After we had been in camp several weeks at Baton Rouge, and had received several mails from home, I saw a little Irish fellow, Pat Conley, looking sad and disconsolate, while the others were reading their freshly received letters. I asked him if he had not received any letters.

He replied, "No. There is no one to write to me. I never had a letter in my life."

"Have you no relatives?" I asked.

"No," he said, "not one."

I learned his story, and took care ever afterward to have a kind word for him whenever I met him, which he repaid with the affection of a warm and generous nature. If when on guard or picket he was able to secure a canteen of milk or some fresh eggs, he was careful to see that the chaplain had a share.

On the night after the battle at Irish Bend I secured a length of rail fence for my own use, while the rest was speedily turned into kindling wood, to cook the coffee. I took off the top rails and laid them over the bottom ones to secure a shelter for the night. When thus employed, Pat came up and said he was looking for me, as he had heard I was sick and without any blanket. I was a good deal used up, and my blanket and horse had been left behind and would not be up for a day or two. Pat at once offered to share his blanket with me. I declined, as kindly as I could. Pat was not neat, and I knew that if I accepted his offer to share his blanket, I should have more bedfellows than I wanted.

As I crawled from under the rails next morning, Pat stood by, waiting to offer to carry my haversack. He had his own gun, cartridge box, knapsack, and haversack to carry. I told him we were to have a forced march that day and he must look out for himself. I had nothing but my empty haversack. It was a hard march. At night our horses came up, and I had a blanket to wrap about me as we lay in an open field.

The next day I found Pat, as our straggling line made its way over the broad plains of western Louisiana. He had confiscated a horse, which he was leading by a rope. Too unselfish to ride, he had piled as many knapsacks of Company B men as he could upon the horse, and thus relieved the tired and footsore men of a portion of their burden. At night Pat's horse and the chaplain's were tied side by side, and shared their rations between them, Pat close by as guard to both.

The next day came an order to have all confiscated horses turned over to the quartermaster. I was eager to save Pat's horse for the good he was doing the company in carrying their knapsacks. While I was meditating how we could save the horse, the quartermaster rode up and ordered the knapsacks off, and the horse turned over to him. Someone near me called out, "That is the lieutenant colonel's horse, sir."

"Well, let him go then," replied the quartermaster.

It was a stretch of the truth, but it was not the only time the truth was stretched all it would bear during the war. Pat kept his horse through all that long march, and then turned him over to the quartermaster.

All went well with Pat till the siege of Port Hudson. On the day before the assault of the 14th of June, Pat was made happy by the arrival of two letters which I had caused to be written to him, one by my wife. He showed them to me with great delight. He passed unscathed through the fierce battle of June 14. The next day, as he lay behind a log near the enemy's works, he thought he saw a head he could hit. He fired and, in the excitement, popped up his own head to see if he had hit. A dozen bullets flew at him and one struck him in the forehead and killed him instantly.

The following night, two men crept in to where the body lay. They found in his pockets the cherished letters. That was all. They threw a few shovels of earth over the dead body, and that was the last of the good-natured, affectionate, unselfish, friendless Irish boy, Pat Conley. There was no one at home to mourn his death. I shall always cherish his memory with tender affection.

Chaplain John F. Moors,
52nd Massachusetts Infantry
Camp-Fire Sketches and Battle-Field Echoes

An Incident at Vicksburg

In April all eyes were on the Army of the Potomac and the Army of the Tennessee. On taking leave of my friend, the Honorable Horace Binney, he said, "If on arrival you should want anything for your hospital, let me know and I will show your letter to Doctor Henry Bellows, the president of the Sanitary Commission."

We had everything but ice and so I wrote. Ice was bought at St. Louis and Chicago, all that could be had. . . . It was placed in lighters and covered with straw and tarpaulins and arrived safely at our landing on the Yazoo River.

During the siege, the sutlers were selling too much ale and beer to our troops. General Ulysses S. Grant ordered that no beer or ale should be sold within sixty miles of our camp around Vicksburg. The ale vendors went away, but returned and located themselves in a swamp beyond the Mississippi, but within five miles of General William T. Sherman's right wing. Our men swam the river at night to gratify their love of ale.

Lieutenant Colonel James H. Wilson, of cavalry fame, was ordered to seize their ale and send them off—much of it was turned over to the medical department. I had more ale at my disposal than any grocery in New York.

One morning I rode up to General Grant's headquarters and pleaded with Dr. J. Madison Mills that I might be permitted to send some of the ale to our men who were working night and day digging the saps and traverses. He said, "Let's go and see

General Grant," and he took me to the general's tent nearby. Lieutenant Colonel John A. Rawlins was with him.

Dr. Mills said, "Dr. Forbes has an idea in his head."

"What is it, Doctor?" said the general.

When I got through, and after some little discussion, Colonel Rawlins said, "But how in the world would you manage it?"

I said, "Just let a subordinate officer or a sergeant go in the trench with a man carrying a bucket of ale with a tin dipper and let each fellow have a dipper full."

General Grant said with a smile, "Well, you may try it; their work is tough in the heat, but be careful."

It was successful. The ration of iced ale was given daily in the trenches. A broad road encircled Vicksburg, close at the base of the Rebel forts, and the saps were now close to the road.

On one occasion, this colloquy occurred. One of our men, in the scorching heat of a June day, saluted the Confederate guard on the top of the largest fort from his trench very near the road. The men were about 150 feet apart. Shaking the iced ale with the dipper in the bucket, he said, "Johnny, do you hear that music? Well, that's iced ale, Johnny."

"You are a liar," screamed out Johnny.

"No, Johnny, we Yanks don't lie. Now I tell you, Johnny, don't shoot and I'll give you a drink. I will go out in the middle of the road and I will put the bucket down and you may come and get it."

"I won't shoot if you bring the ale."

"Done."

At once the Federal soldier mounted out of the trench and, taking the bucket of ale, walked unarmed out to the middle of the road and, putting it down, turned to the Confederate and said, "Now, Johnny, I know you are thirsty; come and get the ale." (At the same time rattling the ice in the bucket.) "But Johnny, if you don't bring this bucket and the dipper back and put it in the road, damn you, I'll have your scalp in less than a week. Now come and get the ale; I won't shoot."

The thirsty fellow left the fort without his musket and came to the bucket and picking it up began to drink. A shout went up from

The Trenches at Vicksburg

the fellows on the parapet who had heard the colloquy. "Bring that bucket here or I will blow your brains out."

He took the bucket to his thirsty comrades. Very soon it was brought back with, "Thanks, Yank, here is your bucket. Come and get it. I won't shoot."

In the annals of war was there ever such an episode? Who but Americans could act thus? Remember one knew he was fighting for the salvation of his country, the other knew he was striving to destroy that country.

Random Acts of Kindness

The one offered his thirsty adversary, in the face of both armies, a refreshing drink of cool ale on a hot day in June, with the thermometer at ninety-five degrees in the shade, and placed the ale where his friend, the enemy, could safely get it. The actors were men from the ranks. . . .

Do you wonder that such men, endeared to one another by such acts, after they had settled satisfactorily the difficulty for which they were in arms, should come together in a union more firm than ever?

Major William S. Forbes,
Medical Director, 13th Army Corps
MOLLUS Papers

General Grant and the Teamster

During the greater part of the siege of Vicksburg my duties were at Grant's headquarters, and I was there enabled to observe some things of that remarkable man which greatly impressed me.

One day, as he was passing a mule team on the line, the driver was beating and cussing one of the mules, and was ordered to quit. But the general, as was his custom, wore simply a blouse without any distinct mark indicating his rank, and for that reason the driver, doubtless supposing he was a mere meddler, turned and began to swear at him. Thereupon Grant directed his orderly to arrest him and bring him to headquarters, where I was ordered to punish the man and tied him up by the thumbs.

When the poor driver found himself in this condition, he was completely subdued and very penitent. He had not dreamed until that moment that it was the commanding general whom he had insulted and refused to obey. He was soon released, however, and by the general's orders taken to his tent, where the fellow was properly reprimanded, not for his insubordinate and insulting language to the general, but for his cruelty to the mule. He insisted upon apologizing for his language and very honestly protested that he did not know he was talking back to General Grant.

Random Acts of Kindness

The general replied in substance, "That makes no difference. I could defend myself, but the mule could not."

Captain Jacob W. Wilkin,
130th Illinois Infantry
MOLLUS Papers

General Ulysses S. Grant

They Were So Hungry

During a rapid advance up the Valley of Virginia, near Winchester, we had a little flour in my mess and nothing to cook it with; so I agreed to slip through our advance line and cautiously approach a farmhouse.

I entered the dwelling with my sack of flour, which was three days' rations for three of us. The lady and three little children met me and said that Yankees had just gone, after robbing the place entirely and burning what they could not carry off. She and the little children had nothing whatever for dinner. I asked her to cook the flour, and with tears rolling down her cheeks she agreed to do so. The little children were so glad to see the flour, as they were so hungry, and this was more than my heart could bear. So I emptied the sack on the table and kissed the little ones good-bye.

The lady followed me to the gate, begging me not to leave my three days' rations. My heart was too full to reply; but in my hasty retreat I turned and said, "Keep it all. We can capture more tonight from the commissary."

Well, one of my daring messmates, named Woodruff, did find something that night. Of course I asked no questions, but thought Colonel Benjamin G. Humphreys went on the march hungry. I was then a boy—am now sixty-eight years old. Those three little children, if living, doubtless remember the incident. God bless the ladies of Virginia! They certainly saw the horrors of Yankee infamy.

Sergeant Wilbur F. Phares,
21st Mississippi Infantry
Confederate Veteran

"I Am the Man, Sir"

Returning from the banks of the Susquehanna, and meeting at Gettysburg, July 1, 1863, the advance of Lee's forces, my command was thrown quickly and squarely on the right flank of the Union army. A more timely arrival never occurred. The battle had been raging for four or five hours. The Confederate general, James J. Archer, with a large portion of his brigade, had been captured. Henry Heth and Alfred M. Scales, Confederate generals, had been wounded. The ranking Union commander on the field, General John F. Reynolds, had been killed, and Winfield Scott Hancock was assigned to command.

The battle, upon the issue of which hung, perhaps, the fate of the Confederacy, was in full blast. The Union forces, at first driven back, now reinforced, were again advancing and pressing back Lee's left and threatening to envelop it. The Confederates were stubbornly contesting every foot of ground, but the Southern left was slowly yielding. A few moments more and the day's battle might have been ended by the complete turning of Lee's flank. I was ordered to move at once to the aid of the heavily pressed Confederates.

With a ringing yell, my command rushed upon the line posted to protect the Union right. Here occurred a hand-to-hand struggle. That protecting Union line, once broken, left my command not only on the right flank, but obliquely in rear of it. Any troops that were ever marshaled would, under like conditions, have been as surely and swiftly shattered. There was no alternative for General Oliver O. Howard's men except to break and fly, or to throw down their arms and surrender. Under the concentrated fire from front and flank, the marvel is that any escaped.

In the midst of the wild disorder in his ranks, and through a storm of bullets, a Union officer was seeking to rally his men for a final stand. He, too, went down, pierced by a minie ball. Riding forward with my rapidly advancing lines, I discovered that brave officer lying upon his back, with the July sun pouring its rays into his pale face.

He was surrounded by the Union dead, and his own life seemed to be rapidly ebbing out. Quickly dismounting and lifting his head, I gave him water from my canteen, asked his name and the character of his wounds. He was Brigadier General Francis C. Barlow, of New York, and of Howard's corps. The ball had entered his body in front and passed out near the spinal cord, paralyzing him in legs and arms. Neither of us had the remotest thought that he could possibly survive many hours. I summoned several soldiers who were looking after the wounded, and directed them to place him upon a litter and carry him to the shade in the rear.

Before parting, he asked me to take from his pocket a package of letters and destroy them. They were from his wife. He had but one request to make of me. That request was that if I should live to the end of the war and should ever meet Mrs. Barlow, I would tell her of our meeting on the field of Gettysburg and of his thoughts of her in his last moments. He wished me to assure her that he died doing his duty at the front, that he was willing to give his life for his country, and that his deepest regret was that he must die without looking upon her face again. I learned that Mrs. Barlow was with the Union army, and near the battlefield. When it is remembered how closely Mrs. Gordon followed me, it will not be difficult to realize that my sympathies were especially stirred by the announcement that his wife was so near him. Passing through the day's battle unhurt, I dispatched at its close, under a flag of truce, the promised message to Mrs. Barlow. I assured her that if she wished to come through the lines she should have safe escort to her husband's side.

In the desperate encounters of the two succeeding days, and the retreat of Lee's army, I thought no more of Barlow, except to number him with the noble dead of the two armies who had so gloriously met their fates. The ball, however, had struck no vital point, and Barlow slowly recovered, though this fact was wholly unknown to me. The following summer, in battle near Richmond, my kinsman with the same initials, General J. B. Gordon of North Carolina, was killed. Barlow, who had recovered, saw the announcement of his death, and entertained no doubt that he was the Gordon whom he had met on the field of Gettysburg.

To me, therefore, Barlow was dead; to Barlow, I was dead. Nearly fifteen years passed before either of us was undeceived. During my second term in the United States Senate, the Honorable Clarkson Potter, of New York, was a member of the House of Representatives. He invited me to dinner in Washington to meet a General Barlow who had served in the Union army. Potter knew nothing of the Gettysburg incident. I had heard that there was another Barlow in the Union army, and supposed, of course, that it was this Barlow with whom I was to dine. Barlow had a similar reflection as to the Gordon he was to meet.

Seated at Clarkson Potter's table, I asked Barlow, "General, are you related to the Barlow who was killed at Gettysburg?"

He replied, "Why, I am the man, sir. Are you related to the Gordon who killed me?"

"I am the man, sir," I responded.

Random Acts of Kindness

No words of mine can convey any conception of the emotions awakened by those startling announcements. Nothing short of an actual resurrection from the dead could have amazed either of us more. Thenceforward, until his untimely death in 1896, the friendship between us, which was born amidst the thunders of Gettysburg, was greatly cherished by both.

Brigadier General John B. Gordon
Reminiscences of the Civil War

1863

On the Field at Gettysburg

I was in the battle of Gettysburg myself, and an incident occurred there which largely changed my views of the Southern people. I had been a most bitter anti-South man, and fought and cursed the Confederates desperately. I could see nothing good in any of them. The last day of the fight I was badly wounded. A ball shattered my left leg. I lay on the ground not far from Cemetery Ridge, and as General Lee ordered his retreat, he and his officers rode near me. As they came along I recognized him, and, though faint from exposure and loss of blood, I raised up my hands, looked Lee in the face, and shouted as loud as I could, "Hurrah for the Union!"

The general heard me, looked, stopped his horse, dismounted, and came toward me. I confess that I at first thought he meant to kill me. But as he came up he looked down at me with such a sad expression upon his face that all fear left me, and I wondered what he was about. He extended his hand to me and, grasping mine firmly and looking right into my eyes, said, "My son, I hope you will soon be well."

If I live a thousand years, I shall never forget the expression of General Lee's face. There he was, defeated, retiring from a field that had cost him and his cause almost their last hope, and yet he stopped to say words like those to a wounded soldier of the opposition who had taunted him as he passed by! As soon as the general had left me, I cried myself to sleep there upon the bloody ground.

Undated newspaper clipping,
Quoted by Long's *Memoirs of General Robert E. Lee*

General Robert E. Lee

Lee's Regard for Private Property

As Lee's army was retreating from Gettysburg, . . . and had reached the plateau of the Blue Ridge, south of Fairfield, Pennsylvania, General Richard S. Ewell was in the valley below fighting the advance. Commissary Sergeant Allis, of General James Longstreet's corps, was driving a herd of beef cattle for that command. Knowing the road would soon be filled with wagons and artillery, he tore down a fence and drove the cattle into an adjoining wheat field.

General Lee, who happened to be there, observed it and asked the sergeant why he wished to destroy that wheat. General Lee told him to put his cattle across the road in some woods where they would "not destroy anything." Although the owner might be an enemy, we were not making war on individuals, and added, "That wheat may be necessary to feed women and children. We cannot afford to be vandals because they have been."

Captain D. L. Sublett,
General John B. Hood's staff
Confederate Veteran

An Act of Mercy

We had routed the enemy at the battle of Jackson, Louisiana, . . . and coming back over the battlefield, I found a large Yankee soldier lying on the ground, groaning. I stopped and looked down at him, when he said, "My friend, will you give me a drink of water?"

"Certainly," I replied, and stooped down and raised his head to my canteen. As I laid him back, he asked me to stay with him till he died. I told him I would, but hoped he was not mortally wounded, then sat down and took his head in my lap. He asked me to get a package from his coat pocket, which I found to be a daguerreotype of a lady and two small children, which he said were his wife and babies. He tremblingly pressed the picture to his lips and asked me to get it to his colonel, to be sent to his wife with the message that he died doing his duty. I promised that I would, but had no idea how I could do so. He had ten or twelve dollars in his purse, which he wanted me to keep, but I told him I would send that also to his wife.

This promise worried me for two days, when I rode out of camp and through the woods till I reached the Yankees posted at Port Hudson, some fourteen miles away. After the usual tests, I was taken to the lieutenant in charge of the reserve post, who sent me on to the colonel's headquarters. The latter treated me very kindly and said he would send the purse and money to the soldier's wife, with his message. He then put his hand on my shoulder and said, "My lad, are you a soldier?" and "To what company do you belong?"

I told him "Company C, . . . Colonel Frank Powers' regiment, General John Scott's brigade—Company C known as McKowen's Scouts."

He said, "Oh, yes, I know you boys, and have met you many times on the battlefield, and know you are daredevils."

In bidding me good-bye, he said, "My lad, if you are ever captured in this part of the army, send for me; I'll take care of you," to which I replied, "You are never going to get me."

Private John Wesley Dixon,
Powers' Louisiana and Mississippi Cavalry Regiment
Confederate Veteran

"I Have Never Forgotten You"

Another raid under Colonel Edward M. McCook. Came while we were at breakfast. Uncle Tom went to the spring to water his horse, not knowing they were in town, and they took the animal from him. Tom started telling them how old he (the horse) was and so on, when a "loyal" citizen stepped forth and told the Federals that he was one of the best pulling horses in town; that he had once owned him and that he would do first rate for artillery or a wagon horse.

Notwithstanding his loyalty, they took the three best horses he had before they left. Sent Eddie before dinner to the provost, Captain Charles C. McCormick, to ask for him (the horse), but he told Eddie the matter would have to be investigated.

About eleven o'clock the doorbell rang and, upon opening the door, Major James W. Stewart and a lieutenant and five other Federals presented themselves.

"We have come to search your house, madam."

"For what purpose?" I asked.

"For soldiers, madam."

"Your search will be fruitless, for I assure you upon the honor of a lady that there are no soldiers concealed here."

"But you will not object to the search?"

"Certainly not, sir, but I should greatly prefer that you should take my word for it."

"I wish we could, madam, but it is your husband. Soldiers,

make a thorough inspection. . . ."

The soldiers reported that they found no one. They then adjourned to Colonel Stephen W. Harris', searching his house thoroughly and telling him that a white man had told them that my husband, Colonel William D. Chadick, was concealed in his cellar. After dinner, some of my friends advised me to go myself and ask for the horse.

We found Captain McCormick's office occupied by three or four Union men. . . . Upon stating the case to Captain McCormick, he said, "Mrs. Chadick, your case is somewhat different.

"Why, what have I done?" I asked.

"Nothing, madam, but your husband has."

Upon his allusion to my husband, I was a good deal excited and although I knew to keep down my emotions, my eyes would fill with tears. Said I, "My husband is a patriot and acts upon principle. He is not like some men you find here in Huntsville— one thing when your army comes along and another when the Rebel army is present. He is a consistent man and, as a soldier, you ought to respect him for it."

"I do, madam. I honor him for it and have very little use for any other sort of a man, but when your army invades the North, you will try to cripple us all you can in taking property, horses, et cetera. So with us when we come here, and as your husband has taken an active part in the war, he must expect to suffer with others. Besides, we have been informed today that your husband has sent off nearly all his property."

"You have been informed, sir, of what is not true," I replied. "I have nothing to conceal. We have sent off some bedding and other articles, with the expectation of moving, and my husband has taken away his fine saddle horse. Had it been his horse you took today, I should never have asked for it, but you do not make war upon women. The horse I asked for belongs to me and I value him chiefly because he is old and gentle and I can drive him myself in a buggy."

"Well, madam, I wish I could give you your horse, but orders are so strict that I cannot transgress them."

I thanked him and told him that I did not wish him to do anything that would interfere with his sense of duty. He followed me out of the room and urged me to go to Colonel McCook, as he was certain he would let me have the horse.

The headquarters of McCook were in the house of Dr. Charles H. Patton. The colonel received me very politely and said, "Mrs. Chadick, I have this moment received a note from Captain McCormick, asking me to come and look at your horse, and if it is in my power, I will restore him to you. I was just about to start."

He then entered into conversation and Mrs. Frederic A. Ross asked him where he was from. He said it was Steubenville, Ohio. I remarked that I had once lived in that town.

"What was your name before you were married?" he asked.

"Miss Cook," I told him.

"Not Miss McCook?" he asked, and said that he expected I dropped the Mc when I came south. I laughingly repelled the charge, and he resumed the questions.

"Did you have three brothers, Dave, George, and Pard?"

I nodded.

"Did you not have a sister, Jane?"

I replied that that was my name.

"I thought your countenance was strangely familiar to me. When I was a boy, you kept me from being put in jail, and I have never forgotten you."

I remembered him very well, but had forgotten the circumstances. He soon recalled it to my recollection. A funeral procession was passing, when several little boys, himself and one of my brothers among the number, got into a fuss and made a great noise in the street. It was near the jail. The constable came out and was going to shut them all up in it, to frighten and punish them. I was looking out of the window, saw it all and went to the rescue.

The boys were crying and thought they all were disgraced forever, and, with difficulty, I begged them off.

He said also that I had whipped him once when in a fight with my brother, and that I was the only Rebel that had ever whipped him. Too, that I should have my horse, and expressed much regret that my house had been searched and said that it was unauthorized by him; that he supposed it was some staff officer who had taken it upon himself.

Mrs. William D. Chadick
Alabama Historical Quarterly

How Confederates Treated a Federal

I was a member of the 93rd Regiment of Ohio Volunteer Infantry. In the battle of Chickamauga, just at dark on Saturday, the 19th of September, 1863, my leg was broken by a musket ball sent out by the Johnnies in our front. This occurred in the woods about a half-mile to the west of Jay's Mill, and we were falling back at the time.

Soon after our lines had fallen back, the Confederates established their pickets for the night. A squad (five, if I remember correctly) was passing to the front about fifty yards from where I had fallen. I called to them. They halted and asked who I was and what I wanted. I replied that I was a wounded Federal soldier and wanted to be helped into an easier position, as I was suffering from a broken leg. They came to me promptly and assisted me as gently as if I had been one of their own men, or a brother, to a large tree where I would be protected from the fire of our own men, first taking off my woolen blanket and spreading it down for me to lie on, placing my cartridge box under my head for a pillow, and spreading my oilcloth over me.

The tenderness with which they had lifted me touched me and I said, "Boys, an hour or two ago we were engaged in shooting each other, and now you are treating me with the greatest kindness. I hardly know how to thank you for it in return."

They only replied, "Well, old fellow, we are doing to you only as we should like to be done by. It may come our turn next," and they passed on to the front picket line for the night.

I was suffering so at the time that I did not notice all of the little details connected with this visit of the Johnnies that night; but the next morning, when I awoke from a half-feverish, dreamy sleep, I found that one of them had spread half of a homemade calico quilt over me, saying nothing about it and doubtless keeping the other half to shelter him in his nightlong watch on picket post.

Was there ever a more beautiful type of chivalry and Christian charity than this? This incident grows brighter to me as the years go by. God bless you, boys, wherever you may be!

Private William C. Brown,
93rd Ohio Infantry
Confederate Veteran

My Johnnie Friend

I desire . . . to mention an incident that occurred in the battle of Chickamauga on Sunday, September 20, 1863, hoping thereby to hear from my Johnnie friend. I was well to the left of General George H. Thomas' corps. The Confederates had attempted to execute a flank movement and were driven back.

About noon there was a lull in the battle, and I concluded to go to the rear in search of water. In passing through the woods we had been fighting over I came upon a wounded Confederate soldier sitting against a tree. When asked where he was wounded he pointed to his knee and said that he was bleeding to death, and asked me to get a surgeon for him. I told him that was impossible. Then he asked me for a drink of water. That, of course, was useless, as my canteen was empty. He said, "Then I reckon I will have to die."

His voice was so weak that he could hardly speak above a whisper. He was a large, fine-looking, and intelligent young man. I looked at the poor fellow and wondered if by any means I could save his life. Ripping his pants' leg up from the bottom, I discovered that the ball had entered from the inside of the left leg just above the knee and cut the main artery, but only made a small rupture. This I could tell by the flow of the blood. I said to him that I was not a doctor, but thought I could stop the bleeding, so I cut a piece out of his pants about two inches wide and a foot and a half long, rolled it up in a tight roll, pressed on the limb above the wound until I got on the artery, then laid the compressed bandage along on the artery, took a silk handkerchief out of my pocket and bandaged the limb tightly. I then asked him if he was hungry. He was, of course, and I sat down with him, and we ate dinner of raw pork and hardtack, but it was good. The hemorrhage was stopped.

Four hours afterwards, in our retreat, I passed the same tree and he was still sitting there. I said, "How do you feel now, Johnnie?"

He looked up and said, "All right. I hope you will get out safely."

This was the last I ever saw of him. Should like to hear from him if living. He will doubtless remember the incident. Someone may ask how I happened to have a silk handkerchief in my pocket. Well, it belonged to the mounted officer who commanded the Confederate column that made the flank movement. He was neither killed nor wounded that I know of, but I got his silk handkerchief all the same, and if he wants it he shall have to call on my Confederate friend.

> Sergeant Harmon M. Billings,
> 86th Indiana Infantry
> *Confederate Veteran*

"It's All I Can Do"

At the time of my capture I was nineteen years of age, and was 1st Sergeant, Company E, 2nd Ohio Volunteer Infantry, . . . 14th Army Corps, Army of the Cumberland.

Many of you are too familiar with the details and incidents of the battle of Chickamauga to need any attempted recital or description on my part. It ended in disaster, and to me the bitterness of defeat was deepened by the gloom of captivity. . . .

I and my fellow prisoners were started on the way to Dalton, Georgia. We had not gone far when we were reinforced by another large batch of prisoners amongst whom I recognized quite a number of the men of my own company. Fortunately their haversacks had not yet been taken from them, and I was able to get some bacon and hardtack to satisfy my hunger. . . .

We reached Dalton about noon, and were there packed into dirty stock cars and at once started for Atlanta. Our guards were changed here, and a regiment of Georgia militia placed in charge. . . . We did not reach Atlanta until the next day, and after some time were taken from the cars and marched to a kind of stockade prison, where we had rations of bacon and cornmeal issued to us, and were told that we would remain for some time.

During the afternoon a raid was made upon us, and the few effects we had left, including our blankets and some of our clothing, were taken from us. I considered myself fortunate in having my blanket only taken from me, as some of the men had their blouses and even their trousers taken, and were compelled to put on the cast-off clothing of the raiders. . . .

A gloom settled down upon us, and for the first time we lost hope and courage, as the full realization of our position and its possibilities dawned upon us. My depression was very great, and it was with a heavy heart that I lay down to sleep.

Early the next morning we were awakened and told to "fall in" for rations, and we were given to understand they were to last until we got to Richmond. . . .

The journey was uneventful, each day a repetition of the others. We passed through Augusta, Branchville, Columbia, Salisbury, Raleigh, and Petersburg, arriving at last at Richmond one evening after dusk. We were taken at once from the cars and marched to one of the military prisons, called at that time "Castle Pemberton" or "Warehouse Prison". . . .

Happening to be at the head of the column, we were among the first to enter "Castle Pemberton" and were quartered on the first floor. . . . Tired and worn out, I lay down and fell asleep. I awoke in the morning feeling stiff and sore from contact with the hard floor, and looked curiously around my new abode. The room was large and bare, and dreary in the extreme. The building had been a tobacco warehouse, and one side of the room was filled with the old presses. At the farther end were the sinks and a hydrant from which we obtained our water supply. In size the room was about thirty by seventy feet, the walls and floor were foul with dirt and vermin, and into this place were crowded—by actual count—378 men. We had none of the commonest necessary articles for the toilet, such as soap and towels, and were obliged to use our coats and handkerchiefs—those of us who were fortunate enough to still possess them,—to dry ourselves after washing. Under such circumstance, the men soon became indifferent and hopeless as to personal appearance, and our condition soon became disgusting and pitiful in the extreme. . . .

The so-called food generally consisted of water, in which meat had been boiled, with a few fragments left floating in it, that it might, by courtesy, be called "soup." A small ration of bread accompanied

it—about enough to give each man perhaps half-a-pound, and once in a great while, a few potatoes. A few tin cups and plates were given to each mess, and we took turns in using them. . . . Thus the days passed wearily, each day the same dreary round, without one gleam of brightness to lighten the gloom that settled down upon us.

One day a ripple of excitement ran through the room at the news that a Sergeant Bell, of the 18th Regulars, from one of the other floors, had succeeded in making his escape from the ration detail one dark evening, but that he had been recaptured and was to be shot as a spy. It soon died away, however, and we sank again into indifference and gloom.

A few days after this, as we were waiting on the pavement outside the commissary for the other details to come out, my attention was attracted by a singular looking white stone, which I picked up and after examining it and showing it to some of the men, threw it away again. Just then I saw an officer, accompanied by a man in citizen's dress, come out from the Libby Prison office and walk rapidly towards us, the man in citizen's dress talking eagerly all the while. I looked at them curiously, wondering what was the matter, and as they came up to us, to my amazement, the man pointing to me said, "This is the man."

They seized me by the arms and I was taken into the office and ordered to "give up the note" that I had picked up. I replied that I had not picked up any note, and explained what it was, and told them to call in some of the men to corroborate my statement. The man stoutly maintained that he had seen one of the officers confined in Libby Prison throw down a note from a window, and that I had picked it up. I as stoutly protested my innocence, and having grown indifferent,—from the suffering and wretchedness of the past months of imprisonment,—as to anything worse that could befall, I told them to search me and make the most of it. The reply was more forceful than elegant, and the officer in charge, calling in a sergeant and a file of men, said, "We've got a way of dealing with such men as you." He ordered the sergeant to "put this fellow in No. 1."

Up to this moment I had been rather indifferent as to what might happen, but when I saw the sergeant step behind the desk and take down one of four keys which hung upon the wall, the significance of it flashed upon me, and like an incoming wave of the sea, all the wretchedness and indignities of the past surged over me, and my heart sank within me. I had tried hard to be brave and cheerful,—to speak and act as hopefully as possible, for the sake of my fellow captives, when my own heart was heavy as lead. But now the revulsion of feeling was more than I could bear and I felt that I was on the verge of breaking down, but by a strong effort I controlled myself and waited for what was to come.

Lighting a lantern and going in advance, the sergeant motioned to the men, who roughly pulled and pushed me out of the room, and down into the middle cellar underneath the prison. Going to the upper left-hand corner, the guard stopped before a door, that, by the light of the lantern, I could see was strongly barred, and unlocked it.

The door was opened and with an oath I was pushed in, stumbling over something on the floor that I felt was a human being, and the door was locked upon me. The sense of companionship, and that I was not utterly alone in my wretchedness, somewhat comforted me, and in response to the exclamation "Hello! Who are you?" I replied, "Sergeant Abbott, of the 2nd Ohio. Who are you?"

"Sergeant Bell, of the 18th Regulars, and two men of the 74th New York."

Bell was the man whom we heard had escaped, been re-captured, and condemned to be shot. Our stories were soon told. He had gotten as far as Petersburg, had been taken sick, and while hiding in the woods had been discovered by a scouting party of Rebels, brought back to Richmond, and put into this cell. As to the report of his being shot, he knew nothing of it. The other two men had been confined for an attempted escape from some other prison.

Their first inquiry was, "Are you not hungry?" Upon my replying that I was almost starved, they said they had "plenty to eat," and gave me some bread and meat. I asked how it happened they fared so well, and was told to wait and see.

After a while, as we sat and talked, I heard the sound of a bolt pushed softly back and a low "Hist!" Bell grasped my arm and led me to the door, and feeling over it,—the place was dark as night,— I found a small opening, and putting my face near it, something was thrust in which proved to be bread, and a voice, that I at once recognized as a Negro's, asked if we had enough water. Bell said that we had, and closing the opening, the man went away. I was then told that ever since they had been there this faithful Negro had brought them food and water every day.

Every morning our food was brought to us and put through the hole by a guard. The cell was about eight feet square, two sides being built of heavy planks built against the stone wall of the corner of the cellar, which were covered with slime and moisture. One corner was foul with filth, and the whole place alive with vermin. We passed the time in sleeping and talking. We could see nothing,—it was one long night, and could only tell when it was day by the tread of feet overhead and the rumbling of wheels along the street.

One day we were aroused by the tramp of feet outside and the jingling of accoutrements. The door was thrown open, the light from lanterns flashed in the darkness, and we were told to come out. Drawn up in front of the cell was a guard of soldiers, two of them having a colored man between them. We wondered what it all meant, and in answer to our looks of surprise the sergeant, a tall, brutal-looking fellow, said, "This nigger here has been bringing food to you fellows, and we're going to show you how we treat your friends."

A wooden bench was then brought and placed before us, and the sergeant, after stripping the shirt from the poor fellow's back, strapped him securely upon it. Then, taking a rope, he whipped him until his back was a mass of raw and bleeding flesh. The poor wretch did not utter a sound, and, enraged at the courageous endurance which his inhuman treatment could not conquer, the monster seized a handful of salt and roughly rubbed it into the raw wounds his cruel lash had made. A low moan of agony broke from the lips of his victim, which rings in my ears today, and sick and faint at the horrible sight, we staggered back into the cell, only too glad to shut our eyes to its horror.

The poor fellow, more dead than alive, was taken up, his shirt thrown to him, and he was ordered with a curse to "go about his work." Our hearts were hot with impotent rage at our helplessness to prevent or avenge the brutal act, and we sat in silence, each one wrapped in gloomy and despairing thoughts.

How long we sat thus I do not know,—some hours, probably,—when suddenly the soft slipping back of the bolt of the opening in the door and the familiar "Hist!" broke the silence. I could hardly believe my ears, and in amazement sprang to the door to find the faithful black fellow there with bread and meat as usual. Astounded at his courage and devotion, I begged him to go away and not to come again. His only answer was, "It's all I can do mar'se,—it's all I can do."

He was "only a Negro," but with a soul so heroic that it seems to me it was of such stuff the martyrs were made.

Sergeant William Abbott,
2nd Ohio Infantry
MOLLUS Papers

Bunny

One bright morning I sat in the matron's room of the "Buckner Hospital," then located at Newnan, Georgia. Shall I describe to you this room, or my suite of rooms? Indeed, I fear you will be disappointed, dear young readers, for perhaps the word "hospital" conveys to your mind the idea of a handsome and lofty building containing every convenience for nursing the sick, and for the comfort of attendants.

Alas! During the war, hospital arrangements were of the roughest. Frequent changes of location were imperative, and transportation was difficult. So it became a "military necessity" to seize upon such buildings as were suitable in the towns where it was intended to establish a "post." Courthouses, halls, stores, hotels, and even churches had to be used—the pews being removed and replaced by the rough hospital beds.

The "Buckner Hospital" was expected to accommodate nearly one thousand sick and wounded, and embraced every building for two solid squares. Near the center, a small stove had been appropriated to the matron's use during the day. Here all business relating to the comfort of the sick and wounded was transacted. The store as it stood, shelves, counters, and all, became "the linen room," and was piled from floor to ceiling with bedding and clean clothing. The back "shed room" was the matron's own. A rough table, planed only on the top, stood in the center. With the exception of one large rocking chair kindly donated by a lady of

Ringgold, Georgia, boxes served for chairs. A couch made of boxes, and piled with comforts and pillows, stood in one corner. This served not only as an occasional resting place for the matron, but with the armchair was frequently occupied by soldiers who, in the early stages of convalescence, having made a pilgrimage to my room, were too weak to return at once, and so rested awhile.

Here I sat the morning in question looking over some "diet lists," when I heard a slight noise at the door and soon a little girl edged her way into the room. Her dress was plain and faded, but when she pushed back the calico sunbonnet a sweet, bright face appeared.

She came forward as shyly as a little bird, and stood at my side. As I put out my hand to draw her closer she cried, "Don't, you'll scare him!"

And then I perceived that she held close to her breast, wrapped in her check apron, something that moved and trembled. Carefully the little girl removed a corner of the apron, disclosing the gray head and frightened eyes of a squirrel.

Said she, "It's Bunny; he's mine; I raised him, and I want to give him to the sick soldiers! Daddy's a soldier!" And as she stated this last fact, the sweet face took on a look of pride.

"What is your name, and how did you get here?" I said.

"My name is Ca-line. Unkle Jack, he brung in a load of truck, un'mammy let me come along, an' I didn't have nothin' to fetch to the poor soldiers but Bunny. He's mine," she repeated, as she tenderly covered again the trembling little creature.

I soon found that she desired to give the squirrel away with her own hands, and did not, by any means, consider me a "sick soldier." That she should visit the fever-wards was out of the question, so I decided to go with her to a ward where were some wounded men, most of whom were convalescent. My own eyes, alas, were so accustomed to the sight of the pale, suffering faces, empty sleeves, and dreadful scars, that I did not dream of the effect it would have upon the child. As we entered she dropped my hand and clung convulsively to my dress. Addressing the soldiers, I said, "Boys, little Ca-line has brought you her pet squirrel; her father is a soldier, she says." But here the poor child broke down utterly. From her pale lips came a cry which brought tears to the eyes of the brave men who surrounded her.

"O, daddy, daddy; I don't want you to be a soldier! O, lady, will they do my daddy like this?"

I hastily retreated, leading the tortured child to my room, where at last she recovered herself. I gave her lunch, and fed Bunny with some corn bread, which he ate sitting on the table by his little mistress, his bright eyes fixed warily upon me. A knock at the door startled us, and the child quickly snatched up her pet and hid him in her apron. The visitor proved to be "Uncle Jack," a white-headed old Negro, who had come for "little Missy."

Tears came to my eyes as I watched the struggle which at once began in that brave little heart. Her streaming eyes and heaving breast showed how hard it was to give up Bunny. "Uncle Jack" was impatient, however, and at last "Missy" thrust the squirrel into my hands saying, sobbingly, "Thar you keep him to show to 'em, but don't let nothin' hurt him."

I arose and placed Bunny in the deep pocket of an army overcoat that hung by the window, and there he cuddled down contentedly. Ca-line passed out with a lagging step, but in a few moments ran back and drawing a box under the window, climbed upon it and peeped into the pocket at her pet, who ungratefully growled at being disturbed. She then ran out without a word to me and I saw her no more.

Bunny soon attached himself to me. Creeping into my pocket,

he would always accompany me in my rounds through the wards, and the sick and wounded took the greatest delight in his visits. As soon as I entered the door the squirrel would run up on my shoulder, and from thence jumping upon the beds would proceed to search for the treasures which nearly every patient had saved and hidden for him. His capers were a source of unceasing amusement to his soldier friends. I cannot describe to you how great. The story of little Ca-line's self-sacrifice went the rounds among them, and all admired and truly appreciated her heroism and her love for "the poor, sick soldiers."

Bunny lived happily for a long time. One day, however, as I was passing along the street, he began as usual to run from out my pocket to my shoulder and back again to nestle in his hiding place. Just then, a large dog came by and the frightened squirrel made a vain attempt to reach a tree by the roadside. Failing, he was at once seized and instantly killed. My regret was shared by all the soldiers, who long remembered and talked of poor Bunny.

Fannie A. Beers
Southern Bivouac

A Pair of Mittens

After the battle of Rappahannock Bridge, on November 7, 1863, Colonel Thomas M. Terry and I, being hotly pursued by a party of Yankees, made a hard run for life and liberty, for we had determined not to be taken prisoners. We came to the bank of the Rappahannock River, and Colonel Terry, throwing off his boots and army overcoat, jumped in and struck out for the opposite shore. I could not swim, and the water was so icy cold that I was immediately seized with cramps, so when the Yankees came charging up and covered me with their guns, I threw up my hands and surrendered.

The Yankees fished me out with their bayonets, and as I was wet and shaking with cold, I was ordered to put on the colonel's overcoat and boots, and then marched off to be shipped to prison. Here I remained four months, when I was exchanged. The first person I met on my return to camp was Colonel Terry. I still wore his boots and overcoat. Glancing at the defaced and dirty garment which had, however, served me well in the Yankee prison, he said, "Belcher, did you happen to find a pair of mittens in those pockets?"

"Yes, sir," said I, "and here they are. I knew you thought a heap of them, and they are as good as new."

The colonel took them reverently, and looked very glad to have them back.

"God bless you," said he; "I value these mittens more than anything I possess, for my dear old mother knit them and sent them to me."

Sergeant Alexander Belcher,
7th Louisiana Infantry
Southern Bivouac

Down in Tennessee

After Sherman's march from Memphis to the relief of Chattanooga, in the fertile valley of Elk River, his column having subsisted upon the country through which it passed, many families were destitute of provisions. The guards left to protect the bridge over Elk River, on the line of the Nashville and Decatur railroad, depended upon foraging parties to procure their subsistence.

These parties had so repeatedly called at Mrs. Littleton Upshaw's, a mile or two south of the bridge, that her supplies were reduced so low as to threaten starvation. She saddled her pony and rode alone to the headquarters of the colonel commanding at the bridge, and told him in a polite and bland manner that it was her wish that he would send a couple of wagons to her house and get the rest of her provisions, as she was tired of the daily visits of his foragers. Her husband being away from home, she always felt alarmed when they came there.

The colonel expressed his pleasure at so frank an offer, pronouncing the policy she was pursuing the best that could be adopted by all the Rebel families in the neighborhood. The next day he sent a commissioned officer in charge of a detail of men with two wagons to Mrs. Upshaw's. The lady politely conducted the officer to her smokehouse and corncrib and through every apartment in her dwelling. Nowhere did he find a pound of meat or a dust of meal or flour.

Going to the kitchen, she directed the men to put a single

shoulder of bacon and bushel of corn stored there—all the provisions she had in the world—in their wagons. Turning to the officer, she said, "Now, Captain, you have seen all that is left, and have it in your wagons; please notify the fact to your colonel, and tell him I hold him to his promise not to permit his foraging parties to come here again."

Instead of the colonel being offended, he chivalrously "took in" the lady's condition, and ordered one of the wagons, full-laden with provisions, to return to Mrs. Upshaw's with his compliments and the assurance that should she at any future time be destitute of provisions, upon notifying him of the fact, she should be supplied. The colonel put a restraint upon indiscriminate foraging, and afterward had little difficulty in procuring supplies for his command from those in the vicinity who had a surplus. . . . .

Dr. Samuel H. Stout,
Director of Hospitals, Army of Tennessee
Confederate Veteran

1863

In Winter Quarters at Dalton, Georgia

One day I was a witness to an act of genuine kindness and politeness by General John C. Breckinridge which increased my already great admiration for the man. As I have remarked, everything at Dalton was in confusion, men going hither and thither seeking their regiments, wagons and teams going from one place to another, some loaded, some empty. Couriers were rushing about with orders to various officers.

The center of activity was a very long building at the railroad depot. It was a freight house, and it was packed with supplies which the quartermasters and their assistants were sending out. The platform, at least a hundred yards long, was crowded with busy men. I saw a man, a private, and a rather dilapidated specimen at that, who was inquiring for General Bragg's headquarters, to which he had been ordered to report. All his inquiries seemed unavailing. He was either ignored or answered gruffly. He came to me and asked me to direct him, but I did not know.

Just then an officer, splendidly mounted, rode up. He wore a heavy overcoat that concealed any mark of rank, but I recognized him as General Breckinridge. He dismounted, throwing his bridle to an orderly who attended him. The poor soldier, utterly discouraged, came up to him and timidly asked if he would direct him to General Bragg's quarters. The general replied at once that he could and would be glad to do it, and, taking the private by the arm, he walked with him clear to the end of that long platform through the seething mass of people until, at the far end, he could point out the exact location; and as the private thanked him and saluted, the salute was returned with as much grace and courtesy as if it had been to General Bragg himself.

Chaplain James H. M'Neilly
49th Tennessee Infantry
Confederate Veteran

Number 27 and the Pumpkin Pie

The women of Columbus, Mississippi, had organized a Soldiers' Relief Association, of which Mrs. James W. Harris was president. This association charged itself with the duty of ministering to the wants of Confederate soldiers as far as lay within their power and of nursing the sick and wounded.

Medicine, by reason of the blockade, was hard to get and exorbitantly high, and quinine was contraband. In every storeroom there had been religiously hoarded small stores of tea, coffee, and sugar, against that possible evil day when some member of the family might be taken sick; but when the sick and wounded soldiers began to come in these precious stores were distributed among them. Daily the ladies went to the hospital with delicately prepared food to nourish the men under the direction of the surgeon in charge.

One day Mrs. Harris, making her usual rounds, leaving cheer and comfort in her wake, stopped to chat with one of the "boys" who was then convalescent. Just as she turned to leave her eyes fell upon the occupant of a bed which was empty the previous evening.

"When did he come in, and who is he?" she asked.

"Some poor devil of a Yankee our boys took prisoner. He was brought in with a lot of our men last night. He has typhoid fever, they say, and is bad off."

Mrs. Harris was of an exceedingly gentle, sympathetic nature, and she had three young sons in the army. What if they, too, were sick and in prison? She stepped to his bedside and beheld a long, gawky youth, about nineteen, burning with fever and tossing in delirium.

"Mother, mother, where are you?" was his incessant and piteous cry.

Her eyes filled with tears at the sight of the young fellow who but a few moments ago had been the "enemy," but now was one of her "boys," to be tenderly nursed. She sought the surgeon, a good man, but harassed from overwork and inadequate means for the discharge of the work he had undertaken.

"Doctor, what is the matter with Number 27?"

"Number 27 has typhoid fever, madam," he replied. "It is almost a hopeless case."

"Is there nothing to be done for him, then?"

"Very little, I fear. By the help of stimulants and nourishing food we might pull him through, but, as you are aware, we have none to spare. Our own men will soon be without," and he sighed deeply.

"Doctor, I'm going to take that poor boy in my own special charge, and while there is any food or medicine left he shall share it."

The next day and the next, and for many more long, weary days after, Mrs. Harris and the doctor tended and nursed the prisoner boy from Maine, but he grew steadily worse. His constant cry had been for his mother, but after awhile he came to believe that Mrs. Harris was his mother, and as long as she was near him he was quiet. The days lengthened into weeks, and at last the fever burned itself out, but it seemed also to have consumed the vitality of its victim.

"Is there any chance for him?" Mrs. Harris asked.

"None whatever, in my opinion, madam."

She stooped down and kissed the sick youth's brow; then, sad and tearful, left him to try to lose herself in a round of other duties.

The next day, upon her return to the hospital, she was astonished to hear that her patient was still alive. She hastened to him and found him conscious. "My son," she said, bending over him, "is there anything more I can do for you? Is there anything at all you fancy?"

He was too weak to speak aloud, but she caught his faint answer, "Pumpkin pie."

Thinking she must be mistaken, she repeated her question.

"Pumpkin pie," he whispered, and the effort exhausted him utterly.

She sought the surgeon. "Doctor, you say there is no possible chance for Number 27?"

"None whatever. He will be dead in twenty-four hours."

"Then, doctor, he shall have his last wish. I'm going home and make that pumpkin pie myself."

The next morning Mrs. Harris entered the hospital with a heavy heart. Of course Number 27 was dead.

The doctor said, "Well, madam, Number 27 is better."

"You don't mean it?"

"But I do, and he is asking for more pumpkin pie."

"May I let him have it?"

"My dear Mrs. Harris, after this you may feed him on thistles, unexploded shells—anything. You can't kill that Yankee."

With a lighter heart she sought his bedside. "Well, my son, how do you feel this morning?"

"Better, ma'am. Can I have some pumpkin pie?" The voice was weak, but there was in it a note of strength which had been absent the day before. His skin was moist, his eye clear. Number 27 was better. "I can have it, can't I, ma'am?" his voice quavering with anxious expectancy.

"My boy, I'll send you one directly. But be careful; don't eat too much at a time."

A ghost of a smile played about his pale, shrunken lips as he replied, "I'll try, ma'am."

Not very long afterward Tildy entered the hospital all agiggle, bearing the pumpkin pie. Again he ate greedily and again fell into a refreshing sleep.

So the boy from Maine got well, and he always declared that if it had not been for those pumpkin pies he surely must have died. His gratitude to Mrs. Harris and the love he bore for the sweet Rebel lady who had done so much for him were too great to be expressed in the limited language at the command of the boy from the backwoods of Maine.

Chicago Times-Herald,
Quoted by *Confederate Veteran*

1864

THE WAR DRAGS ON

Random Acts of Kindness

Kentucky Confederates in Kokomo

I was a very sick boy when orders were received by the Confederate prisoners of war confined in the barracks at Ninth and Broadway, Louisville, Kentucky, about January 22, 1864, to get ready to go northward. Consulting my best interests, I would have asked to be sent to a hospital, but not willing to be separated from my friends who had been captured with me, I went with them.

Reaching Jeffersonville, Indiana, we were put aboard a train for Chicago. The weather was intensely cold, and the best passenger cars in use in those days were uncomfortable. The officer in command was a captain in a Kentucky Federal regiment, whose name I am not sure I remember rightly; and as soon as we had found places in the several cars, he went into each, and calling for the sick men, got seats for each of them near the stove, then in the center of the car, and ordered that they should not be disturbed during the trip. He had with him a large basket filled with food, and this he generously shared at each mealtime with the sick boys, none of whom were able to eat the rougher rations issued to their stronger comrades.

Arriving at Kokomo, Indiana, the train, a special one, was delayed for an hour or two, and the captain came into our car and said to the sick, "Boys, come with me; a gentleman who has a store nearby has given permission for you to sit by his stove while we are detained here. Of course, you will not attempt to escape," he added with a smile.

Escaping was of course in the mind of each of us, but none would have taken advantage of the opportunity thus presented, since, being unguarded, we were upon our honor not to attempt to impose upon the soldierly officer who was responsible for our safekeeping.

The merchant received us kindly and gave us seats near his red-hot stove, and in every way endeavored to make us comfortable. Soon several citizens came in to see what a real, live Confederate soldier looked like, and among them the inevitable man of words rather than deeds. This latter individual availed himself of his opportunity to assail us in the most abusive manner, though none of us dignified him by replying to his coarse tirade. We had been born and bred gentlemen, and properly apprehended that this fellow could not insult us.

The proprietor of the store, however, for the time being our host, came to the rescue promptly. "Look here, Bill Jones," he said, "these men are not only defenseless prisoners, but are ill besides. They are in my house by my consent, and as long as they remain here they shall be treated with respect. If you have such a burning hatred for Rebel soldiers, I suggest that you enlist and go to the front, where they can be found prepared to defend themselves. You are a damned coward, else you would not attack these men who are in the hands of their enemy, ill and defenseless. The quicker you get out of here, the better it will be for your cowardly hide."

As Bill Jones slunk out of the room, we clapped our hands in appreciation of the merchant's kindness, and it is doubtful whether any one of us has forgotten the unknown gentleman who so quickly took our part.

A member of the 1st Kentucky (Confederate) Cavalry
History of the Orphan Brigade

Ties That Bind

On February 1, 1864, a demonstration was made on New Berne, North Carolina, by the Confederates, and during the engagement, a number of prisoners were captured. Among them was William M. Kirby, a young lieutenant of Battery K, 3rd New York Light Artillery. A day or two after the engagement, General George E. Pickett received a letter by flag of truce from his West Point classmate, Union General Innis M. Palmer, requesting his good offices for this young prisoner, accompanied by a bundle of clothing and a remittance of $550 in Confederate money.

Pickett sent a trusted courier, Private J. L. Watkins. . . , with dispatches for Captain Edward R. Baird, who was at General Pickett's headquarters in Petersburg, and with instructions to go on to Richmond with the money and clothing for the young prisoner, to be delivered to the proper officer for his use.

The courier, instead of reporting at headquarters in Petersburg or going to Richmond, made his way to Ivor Station, on the Norfolk & Petersburg Railroad. There, having a courier's pass and being well known, he exhibited a letter addressed to a gentleman living beyond the lines, which he said he was instructed by General Pickett to deliver; and by this means he got through the Confederate lines and took refuge with the Federal army.

As soon as General Pickett learned these facts, he sent to the young officer in prison a supply of clothes and five hundred dollars in money. He also wrote to General Palmer by a flag of truce, acquainting him with all that had happened, and regretting that the receipt of the money and clothes had been delayed. At the same time, he made a demand for the surrender of the courier, in view of the facts of the case.

To this demand he received a reply from General Benjamin F. Butler, who wrote:

> Your note to General Palmer fell into my hands. I have found Watkins and he confesses the appropriation of the money, $550 dollars Confederate Treasury notes. . . .
>
> As the money was being sent by you to a U.S. officer, a prisoner of war, I take leave to return you the like amount.
>
> I have the honor to be, very respectfully,
>
> Benjamin F. Butler,
Major General, Commanding

Andrew Johnston
Southern Historical Society Papers
With additional information from the
Official Records of the Union and Confederate Armies

"It Will Just Ruin Our Honor"

The talking and joking, the trading and "swapping" between the pickets and between the lines became so prevalent before the war closed as to cause no comment and attract no special attention, except when the intercourse led the commanding officers to apprehend that important information might be unwittingly imparted to the foe. On the Rapidan and the Rappahannock, into which the former emptied, this rollicking sort of intercourse would have been alarming in its intimacy but for the perfect confidence which the officers on both sides had in their men. Even officers on the opposite banks of this narrow stream would now and then declare a truce among themselves, in order that they might bathe in the little river. Where the water was shallow, they would wade in and meet each other in the center and shake hands, and "swap" newspapers and barter Southern tobacco for Yankee coffee. Where the water was deep, so that they could not wade in and "swap," they sent the articles of traffic across in miniature boots, laden on the Southern shore with tobacco and sailed across to the Union side. These little boats were unloaded by the Union soldiers, reloaded, and sent back with Yankee coffee for the Confederates.

This extraordinary international commerce was carried on to such an extent that the commanders of both armies concluded it was best to stop it. General Lee sent for me on one occasion and instructed me to break up the traffic. Riding along the lines, as I came suddenly and unexpectedly around the point of a hill upon one of the Confederate posts, I discovered an unusual commotion and confusion. I asked, "What's the matter here? What is all this confusion about?"

"Nothing at all, sir. It's all right here, General."

I expressed some doubt about its being all right, when the spokesman for the squad attempted to concoct some absurd explanation as to their effort to get ready to "present arms" to me as I came up. Of course I was not satisfied that this was not true; but I could see no evidence of serious irregularity. As I started, however, I looked back and discovered the high weeds on the bank shaking, and wheeling my horse, I asked, "What's the matter with those weeds?"

"Nothing at all, sir," he declared; but I ordered him to break the weeds down. There I found a soldier almost naked.

I asked, "Where do you belong?"

"Over yonder," he replied, pointing to the Union army on the other side.

"And what are you doing here, sir?"

"Well, General," he said, "I didn't think it was any harm to come over and see the boys just a little while."

"What boys?" I asked.

"These Johnnies," he said.

"Don't you know, sir, that there is war going on in this country?" I asked.

"Yes, General," he replied; "but we are not fighting now."

The fact that a battle was not then in progress given as an excuse for social visiting between opposing lines was so absurd that it overturned my equilibrium for the moment. If my men could have known my thoughts, they would have been as much amused at my discomfiture as I was at the Union visitor's reasoning. An almost irresistible impulse to laugh outright was overcome, however, by the necessity for maintaining my official dignity. My instructions from General Lee had been to break up that traffic and intercourse; and the slightest lowering of my official crest would have been fatal to my mission. I therefore assumed the sternest aspect possible under the circumstances, and ordered the Union soldier to stand up; and I said to him, "I am going to teach you, sir, that we are at war. You have no rights here except as a prisoner of war, and I am going to have you marched to Richmond and put you in prison."

This terrible threat brought my own men quickly and vigorously to his defense, and they exclaimed, "Wait a minute, General. Don't send this man to prison. We invited him over here and we promised to protect him, and if you send him away it will just ruin our honor."

The object of my threat had been accomplished. I had badly frightened the Northern guest and his Southern hosts. Turning to the scantily clad visitor, I said, "Now, sir, if I permit you to go back to your own side, will you solemnly promise me, on the honor of a soldier, that—"

But without waiting for me to finish my sentence, and with an emphatic "Yes, sir," he leaped like a bullfrog into the river and swam back.

Brigadier General John B. Gordon
Reminiscences of the Civil War

General Forrest Among Civilians

Every living soldier of General Nathan B. Forrest's west Tennessee cavalry remembers the 6th Tennessee Federal regiment, commanded by Colonel Fielding Hurst of Purdy, McNairy County, Tennessee, a regiment of cavalry unknown to fame by any gallant deeds or meritorious conduct on the battlefield, and one which the war records of the rebellion alone have preserved from merited oblivion.

It may be truthfully said of this regiment that it did more plundering, burning, robbing, and running, and less fighting, than any regiment in the Federal army, 5th Tennessee Federal Cavalry only excepted.

On one of Forrest's campaigns, from Mississippi into west Tennessee, and soon after leaving Corinth, he learned that Hurst and his regiment had evacuated Purdy; and that before leaving they had laid in ashes the homes of absent Confederate soldiers, also those of a number of citizens who were known to be in sympathy with the South.

Colonel A. N. Wilson's 16th Tennessee Regiment, of our command, and Colonel John F. Newsom's 19th Tennessee, also, were composed of men from McNairy and adjoining counties, and Forrest knew that unless timely steps were taken to prevent it, there would be trouble when he reached Purdy.

When within a few miles of that place he directed me to take a sergeant and five men from his escort, dash on into Purdy, and place a guard around the residence of Colonel Hurst.

On entering the town, blackened walls, lone chimneys, and charred remains of buildings gave abundant evidence of Hurst's cowardly vandalism. Learning from a citizen that his residence was in the suburbs and directly on our line of march to Jackson, we were soon at its front. Dismounting and entering the portico of his dwelling, I tapped lightly on the door with the hilt of my saber.

In a moment or so it was opened by a lady, when I asked, "Is this Mrs. Colonel Hurst?"

She tremblingly answered, "Yes, sir."

I noticed her agitation, also that on opening the door her countenance quickly changed, manifesting on the instant both surprise and alarm.

Hastening to relieve her apprehensions, I said, "We are not here to harm you, but have been sent for your protection. Although General Forrest has not reached Purdy, he is aware of the ruin and devastation caused by your husband's regiment, and has sent me in advance of his troops to place a guard around your house. This guard is from his own escort, and will remain with you until all of our command has passed, and I assure you that neither your family or anything about your premises will be disturbed or molested."

Giving the officer of the guard instructions, I turned to her, and was in the act of raising my cap before mounting my horse, when, brushing away tears she could no longer repress, she said, "Please, sir, say to General Forrest, for me, that this (referring to the guard) is more than I had any right to expect of him, and that I thank him from my heart for this unexpected kindness. I shall gratefully remember it and shall always believe him to be as generous as he is brave."

Returning to the town, I rejoined the general as he was entering the public square, where he halted and was soon surrounded by citizens of the place, among them the venerable father of

Colonel D. M. Wisdom, of our command, who said, "You see, General, the marks of Colonel Hurst's last visit to our town, and you are also aware that a large number of our citizens are Union people, and they are greatly alarmed for fear of retaliation on the part of your command."

Forrest's reply was characteristic and stripped of his habitual way of emphasizing matters: "I do not blame my men for being exasperated, and especially those whose homes have been laid in ashes, for desiring to revenge such cowardly wrongs, but I have placed a guard around the home of Hurst, and others need feel no uneasiness. Orders have been issued to my command that no Union citizen of this town must be insulted, much less harmed, and this order was accompanied by my personal request that it be obeyed to the letter, and I am sure no soldier of my command will disobey the one, or disregard the other. Of one thing, however, the Union friends of Hurst and his cowardly regiment of Tennessee renegades may rely upon. If we ever are so fortunate as to find them just once in my front, I will wipe them off the face of the earth. They are a disgrace to the Federal army, to the state, and to humanity."

Ever after this, whenever it was known that Forrest was on the move, that command stood not on the order of its going. They well knew that whenever they confronted Forrest there would be a long account to settle. . . .

Captain Charles W. Anderson,
General Nathan B. Forrest's staff
Confederate Veteran

1864

A Young Lady of Tuscaloosa

In my old war diary I find the following, dated Friday, April 29, 1864: Our entire division was reviewed this morning on Pike Street, in Tuscaloosa, by General Samuel G. French and Colonel George B. Hodge, of the president's staff. As my battery, the 1st Missouri, entered the city, a very noted incident took place which did us battery boys so much good that we will never cease to remember a sweet girl there.

The battery had halted briefly in front of her home, when the beautiful blonde young maiden of "sweet sixteen" came out to the street, followed by two Negro boys, one with a large silver waiter filled with wine glasses, and the other with a basket filled with eight bottles of homemade wine. She pointed the servants to the first gun at the head of the battery, and ordered them to start there and, going along the line, to give every man a drink.

Our officers were all in a group at the head of the column in conversation with some other officers, and the servants, misunderstanding their young mistress's orders, passed the first gun and made for the group of officers; but the young lady discovered their error in time, called them back, and made them commence with the privates and noncommissioned officers, and when we were served, not a drop was left for our officers.

The servants soon appeared again, bringing their arms full of vegetables, which they distributed to us privates. Our captain soon ordered us to "Forward, march." The young lady then made her servants run after the battery until every one of us got some vegetables. She accomplished her purpose amid the joy and praises of all the men except the officers. We are all proud of that young lady.

Private William L. Truman,
1st Missouri Battery
Confederate Veteran

"You Should Have Some Feeling"

The writer . . . held a humble position on the staff of Brigadier General Joseph R. Davis (nephew of Jefferson Davis), in the Army of Northern Virginia. . . .Early on the morning of May 6th, General Grant, who had massed a heavy force in the immediate front of Davis' Mississippi brigade, opened fire and began a forward movement on our lines at this point. Seeing we were unable to check their advance, Colonel John M. Stone . . . commanding Davis' brigade, sent word to General Heth, the division commander, that he must be reinforced, which brought to our aid a division of Longstreet's corps, led in person by that able lieutenant general. It was at this critical crisis that General Lee appeared upon the scene.

After the enemy had been repulsed on the right, and while our chieftain was awaiting, in painful anxiety, information from our left wing, a courier—a mere youth—came dashing up with a message from Major General Richard H. Anderson, his small pony panting like a deer that had been pursued by a pack of trained hounds. He delivered his sealed message to General Lee in person, who after reading it, and noticing how tired his pony was, said to him, "Young man, you should have some feeling for your horse; dismount and rest him!" At the same time taking from the small saddlebags attached to his own saddle a buttered biscuit, he gave half of it, from his own hand, to the young courier's pony.

This act of consideration for a dumb beast made a lasting impression upon my then youthful mind, and taught me ever since to treat all animals as if they had feelings as ourselves. At the moment it occurred to me, hungry as I was, that he had better have divided his biscuit with the rider of the animal, or myself; but I soon appreciated the motive of his hospitality to the poor beast, and, as before stated, learned a lesson in kindness to animals I shall not soon forget.

Private Walter B. Barker,
11th Mississippi Infantry
Southern Historical Society Papers

Professional Courtesy

After the battle of Sharpsburg, Dr. William A. Robertson, a Louisiana surgeon serving in Stonewall Jackson's corps, was left behind to care for his brigade's wounded. Seeing his efforts repeatedly hampered by the pilfering of Federal camp followers and stragglers, he appealed to Brigadier General Truman Seymour, of the Union army, for protection. Seymour readily granted the doctor's request and also furnished him with supplies the Confederate wounded needed.

A year or so afterwards, while Dr. Robertson was in charge of Lee Hospital, at Columbus, Georgia, he learned General Seymour had been captured and was a prisoner of war at Richmond. A newspaper account stated that guards were good-humoredly guying the general—"borrowing" souvenir buttons from his brilliant uniform, etc., and that he would soon be sent to a prison farther south. Dr. Robertson immediately wrote to Judah P. Benjamin, the Confederate Secretary of State, as follows:

Office Lee Hospital,
Columbus, Ga., May 10, 1864

Hon. J. P. Benjamin,
Secretary of State Confederate States of America

Sir:

I notice among the captures by our forces reported

by telegram from Richmond the name of General T. Seymour, and have thought it my duty to inform the Government through you of his conduct toward our wounded taken prisoners at the battle of Sharpsburg, Maryland, September, 1862.

I was at that time brigade surgeon of General Hays' brigade, and was left, in company with Surgeon J. B. Davis, in charge of 117 wounded, most of them members of General Hays' brigade. We were left in a very destitute condition, but were visited on the next day, after the occupation of Sharpsburg by the Yankees, by General Seymour, who immediately ordered the chief surgeon of his division to turn over to me any and all articles in his possession that I might need for the use of our wounded. During our stay in Sharpsburg, General Seymour visited the hospital under my charge daily, often inquiring if there were any men who would be benefited by a change, and whenever any were pointed out to him he visited General McClellan in person and procured paroles for them to visit Baltimore and remain there until such time as they were able to be carried within our lines. He also supplied those most dangerously wounded with delicacies from his own table and furnished for the use of all a sufficiency of tobacco, thereby mitigating the sufferings of our wounded and exhibiting a most commendable spirit compared with the general brutality of the majority of the officials under whose charge we were placed. I have made this simple statement hoping that the unusual kindness shown us by him will be reciprocated by our Government....

Trusting this statement may receive the favorable consideration of the Government, I am, with feelings of great respect and esteem,

> Very respectfully, your obedient servant,
> Wm. A. Robertson
> Surgeon in Charge Lee Hospital, Columbus, Ga.

Two months later, Dr. Robertson received a letter from General Seymour, who wrote:

> C. S. Military Prison,
> Macon, Ga., June 8, 1864

My Dear Sir:

A copy of a communication from yourself to Hon. J. P. Benjamin, Secretary of State, C.S.A., dated May 10, has been received by the Commandant at this prison, who kindly showed it to me, asking of your Government kind treatment for me on account of certain circumstances that led to our acquaintance originally. It will gratify you, I am sure, to see the endorsements upon your letter. They are as follows:

> Adj.-General: Send a copy of this letter with instructions to Colonel Withers, at Danville, to acknowledge the humanity and soldierly conduct described within, and to provide for the comfort of General Seymour, as far as consistent and practicable, until he can be paroled or exchanged.
> May 23, 1864. (Signed) Jefferson Davis.

I need not assure you that I have been strongly touched by recollections on your part of circumstances that were certainly nothing more than the result of the most ordinary sentiments of humanity towards the unfortunate. You have my cordial and sincere thanks for thus endeavoring to procure a mitigation of the many inconveniences that attend the life of a prisoner of war.

Your Ob't Serv't,
T. Seymour,
Brig. Gen. U.S. Army.

Later that summer, General Seymour wrote again:

Charleston, S.C., July 7, 1864.

My Dear Sir:

Here in Charleston I am much more comfortably situated than at any previous place of confinement in the Confederacy. We have a large private residence, at the west end of Broad Street, with every essential liberty of exercise, fresh air, and salt-water bathing. Our food is not only unexceptional in quality but in quantity. We are permitted to receive from Hilton Head such articles of clothing, etc., as cannot be conveniently obtained here. We are controlled by gentlemen, and not by jailors.

I was long a resident in this vicinity, and do not fail to meet every courtesy and kindness from those who have known me heretofore. I absolutely lack nothing, except the one thing—liberty to go North—that a prisoner of war could expect or desire; and to your prompt and considerate communication to your

Government, I am sure I owe, and my fellow prisoners owe, much of the amelioration that has taken place in our treatment.

T. Seymour,
Brig. Gen., U.S.A.

Compiled from
Official Records of the Union and Confederate Armies
and
Confederate Veteran

Praying With a Dying Enemy

The 10th of May, 1864, was preeminently a day of battle with the Army of Northern Virginia. I know, of course, that the 12th is commonly regarded as the pivotal day, the great day, and the Bloody Angle as the pivotal place, the great place, of the Spotsylvania fights, and that for an hour or so, along the sides and base of that angle, the musketry fire is said to have been heavier than it ever was at any other place in all the world, or for any other hour in all the tide of time. But for frequency and pertinacity of attack, and repetition and constancy of repulse, I question if the left of General Lee's line on the 10th of May, 1864, has ever been surpassed. . . .

When it became evident that the attack had failed, I suggested to the chaplain—who happened to be with the Howitzer guns, . . . that there might be some demand for his ministrations where the enemy had broken over; so we walked up there and found their dead and dying piled higher than the works themselves. It was almost dark, but as we drew near we saw a wounded Federal soldier clutch the pantaloons of Captain James Hunter, who at that moment was passing by, frying pan in hand, and heard him ask, with intense eagerness, "Can you pray, sir? Can you pray?"

The old captain looked down at him with a peculiar expression and pulled away, saying, "No, my friend, I don't wish you any harm now, but praying's not exactly my trade."

I said to the chaplain, "Let's go to that man."

As we came up he caught my pants in the same way and uttered the same words, "Can you pray, sir? Can you pray?"

I bent over the poor fellow, turned back his blouse, and saw that a large canister shot had passed through his chest at such a point that the wound must necessarily prove mortal, and that soon. We both knelt down by him, and I took his hand in mine and said, "My friend, you haven't much time left for prayer, but if you will say after me just these simple words, with heart as well as lips, all will be well with you: 'God have mercy on me, a sinner, for Jesus Christ's sake.'"

I never saw such intensity in human gaze, nor ever heard such intensity in human voice, as in the gaze and voice of that dying man as he held my hand and looked into my face, repeating the simple, awful, yet reassuring words I had dictated. He uttered them again and again, with the death rattle in his throat and the death tremor in his frame, until someone shouted, "They are coming again!" and we broke away and ran down to the guns. It proved to be a false alarm, and we returned immediately—but he was dead, yes, dead and half-stripped; but I managed to get my hand upon his blouse a moment and looked at the buttons. He was from the far-off state of Maine.

It was long before I slept that night. It had been an unparalleled day. The last hour, especially, had brought together elements so diverse and so tremendous, that heart and brain were overstrained in attempting to harmonize and assimilate them. This was the first time in all my career as a soldier that I had heard from a dying man on the battlefield any expression that indicated even so much as a belief in the existence of any other world than this.

What did it all mean? When that Federal soldier and I had our brief conference and prayer on the dividing line between the two worlds, neither of us felt the slightest tremor of uncertainty about it. To both of us the other world was as certainly existing as this, and infinitely greater. Would I ever see him again? If so, would both of us realize that our few moments of communion and of prayer had meant more, perhaps, than all the struggles that day of the great embattled armies? I went to sleep at last that night, as I shall go this night, feeling that it all was and is too much for me, and committing myself and all my perplexities to the One Being who is "sufficient for these things," and able to lead us safely through such a world and such experiences.

Lieutenant Robert Stiles,
Cabell's Artillery Battalion
Four Years Under Marse Robert

Sherman and "Miss Cecelia"

Miss Cecelia Stovall, of Augusta, Georgia, was a great belle and beauty, who played havoc with the hearts of men. She had every advantage of birth, breeding, and wealth, and once, during a trip north, she visited West Point and was naturally accorded much homage and adoration.

Cecelia Stovall Shelman

Among the many cadets who paid court at her shrine was . . . a slender lad who had hitherto remained impervious to "woman's smiles and woman's wiles." But he capitulated, for the dark-eyed southern girl found the key that unlocked the way to his heart, and he gave her a love which was in keeping with the stern violence of his after enterprises when he was known to the wondering world as General William Tecumseh Sherman.

He lost no time in his wooing, and when he offered her his heart and hand she shook her pretty head and said, "Your eyes are so cold and cruel. How you would crush an enemy! I pity the man who ever becomes your foe."

To this he answered, "I would ever shield and protect you."

But she went away to her Augusta home and married Charles T. Shelman, a wealthy planter, . . . who married her . . . and installed her as mistress of Etowah Heights. Time grew on and with it apace came the war. When the proximity of the invading forces necessitated flight, Mrs. Shelman gathered the children and those dependent upon her and sought protection elsewhere.

Late one afternoon, General Sherman and staff rode up to a fine old mansion . . . while his men had begun its pillage and destruction. Merely out of curiosity, he turned to the aged Negro butler, who stood on the front steps with that courtly dignity which the slave so well learned from his master, and asked him who owned the place.

"Mistis Cecelia Stovall Shelman, sah."

General Sherman recoiled for an instant and then asked, "Was she Miss Cecelia Stovall, of Augusta?"

"De bery same, sah."

An order was issued instructing his men to replace every article removed, and when General Sherman . . . rode away, he left a guard stationed about the premises. He left more, a note in the hands of the butler for his boyhood love. She has now in her proud possession a faded, crumpled bit of yellow paper which reads:

> Mrs. Cecelia Stovall Shelman:
> My Dear Madam—You once said that you pitied the man who ever became my foe. My answer was that I would ever shield and protect you. That I have done. Forgive all else; I am but a soldier.
>
> W. T. Sherman

> Maggie Thornton
> Undated newspaper clipping, *Chattanooga Times*

Dividing the Spoils

I met a "Johnnie" a few days ago, and we were talking about the many things we had observed during our service, and I told of experiences on the Atlanta campaign.

A short distance north of where the Confederates made the midnight charge on General Daniel Butterfield's command was a picket post of which I was . . . in charge. One of our boys went out in front of our post prospecting. He soon returned and reported that he saw several hogs, but failed to get one, and insisted that I should go, as I was a pretty good shot with a revolver.

I turned the command over to him and started. I went perhaps only a hundred yards, when I came to Mr. Hog, and in trying to get a shot at him I was standing astraddle of a stump about knee-high. Before I got a chance to shoot, "bang!" went a gun right in front of me, and the ball hit that stump and knocked it to kingdom come. I very suddenly made a right turn, but went only a few steps when a fine porker came running across my path. I shot at it while running and knocked it down, and I know that hog squealed louder and longer than any hog ever did before or since; but I ran up to it and shot it again, this time in the head, killing it instantly.

Just then I heard someone say, "Do you want all that hog?"

I looked up and there, not ten steps away and coming right up to me, was a "Johnnie" soldier, fully armed. I told him "No," and he said, "Can I have part?"

I answered, "Certainly."

He laid down his gun and accoutrements, and with our pocketknives we soon divided that hog, he taking part and going one way and I the other part and going the other way. There were no questions asked and the war was not mentioned. . . .

> Private W. H. Lee,
> 8th Iowa Cavalry
> *Confederate Veteran*

Strange Bedfellows

I enlisted in the Confederate army in Texas in 1861, at the age of sixteen, and went to Missouri and saw my first fighting at Oak Hills, then at Elkhorn Tavern, in Arkansas, after which our command was dismounted and sent across the Mississippi River and was attached to the Army of Tennessee. After taking part in the battles of Farmington, Iuka, and Corinth, we were again mounted, and our Texas brigade, under General L. S. Ross, was assigned to William H. Jackson's division and took part in all the campaigns of that army. It is not the fighting I desire to tell about, so I will skip that and relate my personal experiences in another matter.

Our division was on the left wing of General Joseph E. Johnston's army all the way from Dalton as Sherman flanked us back to Atlanta. It was fight, fight, fight, all day and often at night, and we were nearly worn out. In a hard fight at Dallas, Georgia, my messmate and chum caught a minie ball through his left arm, at which he rather rejoiced, exclaiming, "Got a furlough at last!" That night he persuaded me to go with him to his sister's who lived, he said, about sixty miles south of Atlanta.

I agreed to go with my wounded comrade and see him safe at his sister's, and my captain said, "All right, go ahead and come back as soon as you can." We were given dinings, picnics, parties, and dances until I forgot about there being any war and that my duty was with my command. After about three weeks of pleasure, I came to my senses one morning and told my chum that we must go back, his arm having healed. He replied, "No, sir, not under sixty days for me."

The third day of my return trip I found the citizens of a little town gathering their forces, old men and boys, to meet a Federal raid that was reported coming to burn a bridge at West Point, Georgia. Finding I was a veteran, I was put in command, and with some four hundred old men and boys we formed on the east side of the river and remained all day, when we learned the Yanks had changed their course.

I bade my valiant command good-bye, rode on toward Atlanta, and at a little town (I think Hamilton) I met up with a Lieutenant Black, who belonged to the 3rd Texas, whom I knew well. He had been badly wounded and was returning to his company. I was glad to get with him, as the home guards had several times tried to arrest me. I told the lieutenant where I had been and he said, "All right, we'll go on together."

As dark approached we saw a large two-story house some distance back from the road and concluded to try our luck on getting to spend the night there. We rode up to the gate, and soon a gentleman came out, to whom we explained our wants. When he found out that we were going to the army, he told us to get down, saying that he would gladly take care of us and adding, "Come right in. I'll have your horses cared for."

He took us through the house and out into the dining room, which was detached from the house. Seating us at a table full of good old Georgia victuals, he called a Negro woman and told her to wait on us, excusing himself to go see about our horses. He soon came back and conversed with us about the war and its outcome until we were through eating.

The lieutenant said, "My friend, we will not stay for breakfast, as we are anxious to get to our command; and if you will show us to our place of sleep, we will retire."

"O, I can give you breakfast anyway. We have plenty of Negroes; but I will show you where to sleep."

I had noticed several women and two or three men about the place, but never thought anything about it. "Young man," he said, turning to me, "you go upstairs," designating a room.

On arriving at the top of the stairs I saw a door open and a candle burning on a table in the corner. A Confederate candle was a poor affair for giving light. However, I supposed that room was intended for me. The bed was in the far corner, and I went over to it and saw there was someone in it; but, it not being uncommon to put two soldiers in a bed, I thought nothing about it and, taking off my jacket and pants and shoes, blew out the candle and rolled in. In getting into the bed I rolled against the other fellow on purpose, thinking I'd wake him and let him know I was there also. He didn't move, however, and I turned over and went to sleep.

How long I had been asleep, I have no idea; it might have been but a few minutes or an hour; but I woke up suddenly, hearing voices in the room. Someone said, "Why, who put out the candle?" The candle was relit, and a man and a woman took seats at the table, the woman facing me. I kept wondering what in the world they were doing in the room. I could occasionally hear part of their conversation, but could catch on to nothing that related to me. I could not go to sleep and kept watching them as well as I could from my position and wishing they would get out. Finally the lady said in rather an indignant voice, "You ought to be ashamed to be talking about love in the presence of the dead."

In less time than I can tell it I realized that my bedfellow was dead; that I had got into the wrong room. I knew I was in bed with a dead man, and I didn't intend to stay. Without thinking anything about the consequences, I sat up and looked toward them.

The lady saw me first and, with a scream that, it seemed, would take the roof off the house, she jumped clean out of the room. The man looked toward the bed and, with a yell and a leap, he kicked over the table, and those two people got down those stairs in a hurry. I got out and, gathering up my duds, scampered across the hall into another room (the one intended for me, I guess) and, fastening the door, rolled into bed.

The commotion that was going on downstairs soon had everybody, Negroes and all, aroused. I could hear the women call for camphor and all manner of restoratives, and the men were running about to beat the band. It took some time to find out what was the cause of all the trouble, but finally I heard them coming up the stairs and heard the lieutenant ask where I was. They told him I was in that room, and he made me let him in, and I played off so sleepy that I couldn't understand that a dead man had come to life in the room opposite.

They were all apparently afraid to go in, until the lieutenant said, "Give me the candle. If he is not dead, he needs attention," and in he went. He went up to the bed and found the sheet turned down as I had left it, and said, "Why, the man is dead. The wind just blew the sheet off."

"No sir, that man rose and was sitting up looking at me," exclaimed the man who was in the room when I got up. He doubtless thought so.

There was no sleep for me the balance of that night, and as soon as the chickens began crowing for day I went and saddled up our horses, woke the lieutenant, and we rode off. I have ever since had remorse of conscience for not telling our host before I left how the whole thing occurred.

That day, after we had ridden ten or twelve miles, I told the lieutenant about it under promise of secrecy. He got off his horse and laughed until I got mad and left him, and he failed to keep the secret. He related the incident to General Ross, who used to laugh heartily. One time when he was our governor he got me to relate it to some friends in his office.

We reached the command in the midst of the terrible fight at Marietta, Georgia, and I had shot about twenty times before my captain knew I had returned. He treated me awful nice and never said a word about my long absence.

Private I. E. Kellie,
27th Texas Cavalry
Confederate Veteran

A Friend in Need

At the battle of Cold Harbor, Virginia, June 3, 1864, the 7th New York Heavy Artillery, armed as infantry, were entrenched about eighty yards in front of us. We were on the crest of a ridge; they were below us. Behind us, for supports, were two Delaware regiments, their combined strength being about 120 men.

Back of us was the alder swamp, where springs of cool water gushed forth. The men in front of us had to go to these springs for water. They would draw lots to see who should run across the dangerous, bullet-swept ground that intervened between our earthworks and theirs. This settled, the victim would hang fifteen or twenty canteens around him; then, crouching low in the rifle-pits, he would give a great jump and when he struck the ground he was running at the top of his speed for our earthwork. Every Confederate sharpshooter within range fired at him. Some of these thirsty men were shot dead, but generally they ran into the earthwork with a laugh.

After filling their canteens, they would sit by our guns and smoke and talk, nerving themselves for the dangerous return. Adjusting their burden of canteens, they would go around the end of our works on a run and rush back over the bullet-swept course, and again every Confederate sharpshooter who saw them would fire at them.

Sometimes these water-carriers would come to us in pairs.

One day, two Albany men leaped into our battery. After filling their canteens, they sat with us and talked of the beautiful city on the Hudson, and finally started together for their rifle-pits. I watched through an embrasure and saw one fall. Instantly, he began to dig a little hollow with his hands in the sandy soil, and instantly the Confederate sharpshooters went to work at him. The dust flew up on one side of him, and then on the other. The wounded soldier kept scraping his little protective trench in the sand. We called to him. He answered that his leg was broken below the knee by a rifle-ball.

From the rifle-pits we heard his comrades call to him to take off his burden of canteens, to tie their strings together, and to set them to one side. He did so, and then the thirsty men in the pits drew lots to see who should risk his life for the water. I got keenly interested in this dicing with death, and watched intently.

A soldier sprang out of the rifle-pits. Running obliquely, he stooped as he passed the canteens, grasped the strings, turned, and in a flash was safe. Looking through the embrasure, I saw the dust rise in many little puffs around the wounded man, who was still digging his little trench, and, with quickening breath, felt that his minutes were numbered.

I noted a conspicuous man, who was marked with a goiter, in the rifle-pits, and recognized him as the comrade of the stricken soldier. He called to his disabled friend, saying that he was coming for him, and that he must rise when he came near and cling to him when he stopped. The hero left the rifle-pits on the run; the wounded man rose up and stood on one foot; the runner clasped him in his arms, the arms of the wounded man twined around his neck, and he was carried into our battery at full speed and was hurried to the rear and to a hospital. To the honor of the Confederate sharpshooters, be it said, that when they understood what was being done they ceased to shoot.

Private Frank Wilkeson,
11th New York Battery
Recollections of a Private Soldier

Standing on the Promises

One day there was brought into the hospital a fine looking young Irishman, covered with blood and appearing to be in a dying condition. He was of a Savannah regiment, and the comrades

The Arrival of the Wounded

who were detailed to bring him to us stated that in passing Lynchburg they had descended at the station and, hurrying to regain the train, this man had jumped from the ground to the platform. Almost instantly, he was seized with vomiting blood. It was plain he had ruptured a blood vessel, and they had feared he would not live to get to a hospital.

Tenderly, he was lifted from the litter and every effort made to staunch the bleeding. We were not allowed to wash or dress him, speak, or make the slightest noise to agitate him. As I pressed a handkerchief upon his lips, he opened his eyes and fixed them upon me with an eagerness which showed me he wished to say something.

By this time we had become quick to interpret the looks and motions of the poor fellows committed to our hands. Dropping upon my knees, I made the sign of the Cross. We saw the answer in his eyes. He was a Catholic and wanted a priest to prepare him for death. Softly and distinctly I promised to send for a priest, should death be imminent, and reminded him that upon his obedience to the orders to be quiet, and not agitate mind or body, depended his life and his hope of speaking when the priest should appear. With childlike submission he closed his eyes and lay so still that we had to touch his pulse from time to time to be assured that he lived.

With the morning the bleeding ceased, and he was able to swallow medicine and nourishment, and in another day he was allowed to say a few words. Soon he asked for the ragged jacket, which, according to rule, had been placed under his pillow, and took from the lining a silver watch; and then a one hundred dollar United States banknote greeted our wondering eyes. It must have been worth one thousand dollars in Confederate money, and that a poor soldier should own so much at this crisis of our fate was indeed a marvel.

I took charge of his treasures till he could tell us his history and say what should be done with them when death, which was inevitable, came to him. Though relieved from fear of immediate death, it was evident that he had fallen into a rapid decline. Fever and cough and those terrible "night sweats" soon reduced this stalwart form to emaciation. Patient and uncomplaining, he had but one anxiety, and this was for the fate of the treasures he had guarded through three long years in battle and in bivouac, in hunger and thirst and nakedness.

He was with his regiment at Bull Run, and after the battle, seeing a wounded Federal leaning against a tree and apparently dying, he went to him and found he was an Irishman who belonged to a New York regiment. Supporting the dying man and praying beside him, he received his last words, and with them his watch and a one hundred dollar banknote, which he desired should be given to his sister. Our Irishman readily promised she should have this inheritance "when the war ended," and at the earliest opportunity sewed the money in the lining of his jacket and hid away the watch, keeping them safely through every change and amidst every temptation which beset the poor soldier in those trying days. He was sure that he would "some day" get to New York and be able to restore these things to the rightful owner.

Even at this late day he held the same belief and could not be persuaded that the money was a "fortune of war;" that he had a right to spend it for his own comfort, or to will it to whom he would; that even were the war over and he in New York, it would be impossible to find the owner with so vague a view as he possessed.

"And did you go barefoot and ragged and hungry all these three years," asked the surgeon, "with this money in your pocket? Why, you might have sold it and been a rich man and done a world of good."

"Sure, Doctor, it is not mine to give," was the simple answer of the dying man. "If it please Almighty God, when the war is done I thought to go to New York and advertise in the papers for Bridget O'Reilly, and give it into her own hand."

"But," I urged, "there must be hundreds of that name in the great City of New York; how would you decide should dishonest ones come to claim this money?"

"Sure I would have it called by the priest out from God's holy altar," he replied after a moment's thought.

It was hard to destroy in the honest fellow the faith that was in him. With the priest who came to see him he argued after the same fashion, and as his death approached we had to get the good bishop to settle this matter of "conscience money."

The authority of so high a functionary prevailed, and the dying man was induced to believe he had a right to dispose of this little fortune. The watch he wished to send to an Irishman in Savannah who had been a friend and a brother to him, for he had come with him from the "old country." And for the money! He had heard that the little orphans in Savannah had had no milk for two long years. He would like "all that money to be spent in milk for them." A lady, who went south the day after we buried him, took the watch and the money and promised to see carried out the last will and testament of this honest heart.

> Emily V. Mason,
> Lexington, Virginia
> Quoted by *Our Women in the War*

Compassion for a Confederate

During the Atlanta campaign in 1864, after a hard battle on the 19th of June, near Kennesaw Mountain, the contending parties struggled until darkness covered the mountains, a kindly mantle covering the dead and dying boys in blue and in gray.

Some thousands of us, yet alive, lay there helpless until near morning, when searching parties, under cover of darkness, moved us to the rear. With us was carried back to the field hospital a young Confederate soldier, mortally wounded, and suffering great agony, being shot through the bowels with a minie ball, and he was laid on a cot adjoining mine. He was intelligent and educated. The long campaigns in which he had been engaged had reduced his wardrobe to a low ebb, but through the torn and tattered raiment shone the reflection of the gentleman.

In mortal agony, low moans would escape his faltering lips; and, recovering himself and turning to me, he would apologize for having disturbed me. At every request I made for the attendant to bring him some relief he turned gratefully to me with a gentle "Thank you;" for every cup of water or dose of medication administered the kindly "Thank you" followed.

Knowing that his time for this earth was short, he gave me his name, company, and regiment, and requested that I communicate with his people if I should ever have the opportunity. But before giving their names and addresses he became flighty, and his mind evidently wandered back to his home in Tennessee. Again he lived over the old home life among his kindred and friends; he walked along the shady paths and over the old fields; again he tasted the cold water, which he dipped up with the old gourd as it flowed over the rocks in the dear old springhouse; once more he romped with his sisters and talked with them of father and mother in heaven. Then his mind would revert to the war, would dwell upon the gathering gloom that was spreading over his dear Southland, would picture in feeling terms the loss of some brave comrade and the suffering borne by those who had been brought up in luxury; but for himself no sigh nor complaint ever escaped him. Again, becoming a suppliant at the throne of grace, he thanked his Heavenly Father that it was his fortune to have fallen into the hands of those whom he had looked upon as enemies, but who, in his adversity, had proved to be friends. He fervently implored God to be a father to his orphan sisters and protect them in the days to come. In feeling supplication he asked the Great Ruler to bless his beloved land and the rulers thereof, and prayed that the days of danger and trouble would soon end in peace.

Thus the moments slipped away, and during the dark hours of night his soul went back to his God. Thus passed from my presence through the portals of heaven the immortal spirit of William H. Parks, Company K, 12th Tennessee, C.S.A.

At my request, young Parks was buried in a shady nook in a grave separate and apart from all others, and his lonely resting place marked. I also mapped the vicinity, so that his place of burial could be found in the future should his friends be discovered. In 1869 his remains were disinterred, and now rest with his comrades in the Confederate cemetery at Marietta, Georgia.

Time passed on, and in the spring of 1865 the war was virtually over; and the government, not being able to patch me up for any further use, turned me adrift, a physical wreck, to begin life anew. I endeavored to forget the scenes of those four dark years, and I put as far away from me as was possible all remembrance of those sad times, till one day, several years after, I came across one of my wartime diaries. It brought to mind my promise to the dying Confederate. I wrote letters to a dozen post offices in Tennessee, but could learn nothing. I resolved to try another method, and advertised in the newspapers of Memphis and Nashville. In a few days letters began coming thick and fast from comrades, friends, and relatives. No word had ever reached them concerning his fate. From these letters I learned that young Parks' home had been at Humboldt, Tennessee, and that his two sisters, Mrs. M. P. McIntosh and Mrs. S. E. Northway (now of Waverly Place, Nashville), lived there. A correspondence followed with one of these sisters that continued through several months, and I received some beautiful letters expressive of gratitude in the most devoted Christian spirit for the small service I had rendered.

> Corporal George H. Blakeslee,
> 129th Illinois Infantry
> *Confederate Veteran*

An Incident at Kennesaw Mountain

It has often been a matter of speculation with me why (in the various episodes and sketches of the "late unpleasantness") some truthful account has not been given by the "Northern side of the fence" of the Federal charge on the Confederate line of works at the battle of Kennesaw Mountain, June 27, 1864. It appears to me as a climax to that dreadful and fearful onslaught the Yankees owe the Rebels a debt of gratitude that for over fifty years has lain dormant without the least attempt at acknowledgement. . . .

On the evening previous to the Kennesaw fight a battery of . . . light artillery came up, halting near our command. . . . I should mention that our line was on the brow of a slight eminence, and the Yankee line was also on a slight rise, there being a depression and gully between the two lines, our line and the Federal being in clear view of each other and but about one hundred yards apart. We were assured there would be a red-hot mix-up, and . . . had cut down and placed in our front hundreds of blackjack saplings as abatis, cutting off the tips of the limbs with our jackknives and whittling them so sharp and close it would have been an uphill business for a rabbit to creep through. . . .

I should also mention that in the valley or depression between the lines was a grove of pine and blackjack, the ground being thickly strewn with leaves and pine cones, which were like tinder.

About 10:00 a.m. we could see quite a commotion across on the Yankee side, line after line apparently marching and countermarching. They seemed to be assembling mainly from their rear, massing just behind their breastworks. This meant for us every man to his place and fix for business. Line after line of Yanks mounted their works, and simultaneously their ordnance opened on us. Cannon—big, little, old, and young—made such a din that their muskets sounded like squibs.

If any command was ever given for us to commence firing, I never heard it, but I distinctly call to mind we commenced firing and our . . . battery—gracious Peter! I could have hugged every man in that battery. It sounded as though we had a hundred cannon instead of eight or ten, and such regularity one would think they were on parade drill—scattering canister, grape, shrapnel, and short-fire bombs, and, like our infantry, shot for execution.

Well, the Yanks got as far as the gully in the ravine, which seemed at that time the healthiest place. One would imagine Vesuvius had moved over to the Confederate States of America and opened up business on Kennesaw.

As mentioned, our cannon were placed for execution. Their redoubts so low, the cannon's mouth nearly on the ground, and at every discharge a blaze of fire sprang out among the dry leaves, which were soon ablaze and eating their way toward the gully, which was full of a mass of human beings, squirming around and still piling on each other. Ah, but little can a peaceful citizen imagine the horror of war. Just one glimpse of that seething mass of weltering human beings, the flying, burning sticks with every discharge, flames leaping from limb to limb, the everlasting roar of cannon and small arms, not counting our usual Rebel yell.

At this stage our colonel, Will H. Martin, sang out, "Boys, this is butchery," and mounting our head logs, with a white handkerchief, he sang out to the Yanks as well as to our own men, "Cease firing and help get out those men."

It is needless to add that the Feds never once refused to comply with this request. Our men, scaling the head logs as though for a countercharge, were soon mixed with Yankees, carrying out dead and wounded Feds with those who, a few minutes previous,

Colonel Martin Calls a Truce

were trying to "down our shanties." Together, the Rebs and Yanks soon had the fire beat out and the dead and wounded removed to the Federal side of the fence.

Now, I will say this. The Yankees who were really engaged in this little matter were fully appreciative of our action, and I can't begin to mention the nice things they said to us. A Federal officer presented to Colonel Martin a brace of fine pearl-handled pistols, making quite a feeling little speech, not lengthy but to the point.

But still, after the war was over, and at a time when the bloody shirt was flaunted far and near, at every crossroad public speaking, barbecue, and Sunday school picnic, never once was this little episode of the battle of Kennesaw Mountain mentioned, or any mitigating circumstances that it might be possible for any Confederate to be imbued with human feeling.

How nice it would have been for some Federal soldier, who participated in the grand charge at Kennesaw Mountain, to have mentioned the foregoing facts, not wait for half a century when nearly everyone familiar with the episode is dead and gone.

Private W. T. Barnes,
1st Arkansas Infantry
Confederate Veteran

Unconscious with Kindness

Soon after Sherman's army was so signally repulsed on the Kennesaw line, he again commenced his flank movement, which forced our army to fall back.

On July 4, 1864, one of the hottest days of the season, our army arrived at Vining's Station, just below Marietta, Georgia, where it was formed in line of battle, with orders for each brigade to entrench and throw up breastworks.

I was busily engaged all the morning in superintending the work, which was about completed between twelve and one o'clock, when, with my staff, I retired to a large spreading oak tree, about 150 to 200 yards in the rear of my line of works, to rest and to eat my scanty rations. No fighting was going on at this time except an artillery duel between a Federal battery, some distance off, and a Confederate battery on my line.

After I had eaten up all the rations I had, I concluded I would take a smoke. Matches in those days were very scarce and hard to get, so I always carried with me a small sunglass to light my pipe with when the sun was shining. After filling my pipe, I noticed that the sun was shining through a small opening in the foliage of the tree under which I was sitting, and I remarked to Colonel Beverly L. Dyer, my inspector general, that I could light my pipe through the little opening. He replied that he would bet me a drink of pine-top whiskey that I could not. I accepted the bet (as I was then not as punctilious about betting as I am now), and just as I was in the act of drawing a focus on my tobacco, a shell from the enemy's battery came whizzing through the air over my line and exploded just as it struck my foot and the ground, tearing off my foot and making a hole almost large enough to bury me in.

My staff officers were lying under the shade of the tree, but none of them were struck by the shell or any of its fragments. Colonel Dyer, who was standing over me at the time, had nearly all his clothing torn off, not by the shell or its fragments, but by the gravel that was thrown up against him. He received seventeen flesh wounds, none of which proved very serious. . . .

The shock from the explosion of the shell was very severe, yet the tearing away of my leg was accompanied by neither pain nor the loss of much blood. In addition to the loss of my foot, I received another wound on my other leg, which was rather remarkable. I had a cut below the knee about four inches long and down to the bone, as smooth as if it had been cut with a sharp knife, yet neither my pants nor underclothing were torn. It was so smooth a cut that when pressed together it healed by first intention. None of us were able to conjecture what made this cut. Before I would allow my removal I made my staff find my sunglass and my pipe. The rim of my sunglass was broken.

As soon as it was known that I was wounded, the surgeons of my brigade and division came to my assistance and bound up my wounds as best they could and gave me some morphine and whiskey. I was then put in an ambulance and started to the field hospital. In going to the hospital, I passed by General Benjamin F. Cheatham's headquarters, who, hearing that I was wounded, came out to sympathize with me and suggested that, as I was looking very pale, he thought that some stimulant would do me good and gave me a stiff drink.

I then began to feel pretty good and proceeded on my way to

the hospital. I had not gone very far when I passed General William J. Hardee's headquarters. He had heard of my misfortune and came out to see me. He also said I was looking very pale and that I ought to have some stimulant, and gave me a big drink.

I continued to feel better, and again started toward the hospital, and in a short time passed General Joseph E. Johnston's headquarters. He came out to see me and also said that I was looking very pale, and that some stimulant would do me good. He happened to have some very fine apple brandy, and gave me a big drink, and down it went. From this time on I knew nothing until I awoke on the platform at Atlanta at sunrise next morning.

Brigadier General Alfred J. Vaughan, Jr.
Camp-Fires of the Confederacy

Master and Slave

On the morning of July 14, 1864, a detachment of the 6th Alabama Cavalry, about 115 men, under the command of General James H. Clanton, encountered a largely superior force of Yankee raiders led by General Lovell H. Rousseau at Greensport Ferry, on the Coosa River. Colonel Henry J. Livingston, with about 250 men, was holding back the enemy's main body at Ten Islands Ford. It was imperative for us to hold the road until reinforcements could reach us; otherwise the Oxford Iron Works, upon which the Confederate foundries at Selma, Alabama, depended, would be destroyed.

The men had been well posted behind trees and rocks on the slope of a thickly wooded hill, and the road extended along the river bluff. The firing on both sides was spirited. The enemy, in spite of superior numbers, could not drive our boys from their position; but they seemed determined to gain possession of the road, and they formed a heavy column with which they could pass our thin line and clear the road before them.

General Clanton and two of his staff officers, Captains Robert S. Abercrombie and "Batt" Smith, and also Tommy Judkins, were standing in the middle of the road, dismounted. A few feet away, on the side of the road, were five or six young fellows attached to headquarters and eight or ten boys of the 6th Alabama Cavalry, also dismounted. I was behind a large tree, a few feet in advance of the general, and had a good view of everything in front. A heavy column of the enemy on foot was coming around the curve of the road, about two hundred yards distant. Suddenly, just behind me, I heard a loud, fierce yell, and two staff officers, followed by the headquarters' boys and the small squad of the 6th Alabama Cavalry, dashed at the enemy, who quickly poured a deadly fire upon them and then halted.

Abercrombie and Tommy Judkins were killed. "Batt" Smith and the handful of boys close behind him kept on. In a few seconds, Smith fell headlong upon his face and then turned over on his back. The effect of the enemy's fire was appalling. Not one of that gallant little band was left standing. The charge was reckless in the extreme, but it illustrated the spirit and high courage of our soldiers.

That feat of daring was followed by another of the lowliest and humblest man there present. A tall, strapping, young Negro named Griffin approached General Clanton and asked, "General, where is Marse Batt?"

The general pointed down the road and said, "There, near the enemy's line, dead."

Griffin at once started down the road. He was called back, but did not heed. He sped on in the face of that heavy fire, took up the wounded young officer, and carried him in his arms from the field. He came up the road for a few yards, then stepped into the woods and came out again on the road just where the general was standing.

"Is he dead, Griffin?" asked General Clanton.

"I don't know, sir," he replied. "Mammy was his nurse, and I am the older. I promised mammy to take care of him and to bring him back to her, and I am going to carry him home."

Simple words, but how much do they convey! An untutored Negro slave carrying out his mother's commands in behalf of her nursling at the risk of his own life! I have often thought of that day, and the scene is vivid. I can see the deathly pale face of the unconscious and sorely wounded young officer as he was being carried to safety in the arms of his faithful slave. . . .

Private Samuel Coleman,
6th Alabama Cavalry
Confederate Veteran

A Night on the Battlefield

Near Winchester, Virginia, on the afternoon of July 20, 1864, a Confederate force under General Stephen D. Ramseur was defeated by Federal troops under General William W. Averell. The Confederates were compelled to beat a rapid retreat and left their dead and wounded on the battlefield.

As night came on, a number of women of Winchester arrived on the scene to give aid and comfort to the wounded. Among the young girls who had thus volunteered was Miss Tillie Russell. In passing among the dead and wounded, visible by the light of the moon and the lanterns of the Federal surgeons, Miss Russell came upon a youth suffering the greatest agony. He was Randolph Ridgely of Maryland, although she then knew only that he was a Confederate soldier. His clothing was soaked in the blood from his wound, which, some time before, had been hastily dressed by the Federal surgeon. Miss Russell raised Ridgely's head to give him, if possible, some ease, whereupon the wounded man gave a sigh of relief and his head sank back into her arms as she sat down beside him. Almost at once, his low moans gave place to regular breathing as he fell into a sleep of exhaustion.

After some time, Miss Russell found herself and her charge alone on that portion of the field among the dead and wounded. She attempted to change the position of the wounded man and free herself from a severely cramped position, which, all the while, grew more and more painful. Whenever she attempted to move, however, the soldier moaned and awoke. The Federal surgeon who had dressed young Ridgely's wound came by and told her that the case was critical, but that if the wounded man could sleep until morning, he might live. On the other hand, his fever was at its most dangerous point, and if his sleep were broken, he would die. Then and there, regardless of her own suffering, Tillie Russell resolved to make no further effort to lay Ridgely's head on the grass, but would support his head until his life should be assured by the rest he needed.

Hour after hour went slowly by. The moon passed through the heavens, and there was no sound on the battleground except that of a fitful breeze in the nearby woods. The girl was suffering agony, but she never faltered! At the first touch of dawn, she saw the soldier awake with a faint smile on his lips. Forgetful of self, her feeling was one of thankfulness that she had saved the life of a Confederate soldier.

Miss Russell was made seriously ill by her experience, and she could not lift her hand for some days. The story of her deed was eagerly sought for publication, but she refused permission to have her name used in connection with it. Artists visited the scene and portrayed the incident with brush and pencil. . . . It should always be associated with the memory of one of the most unselfish and self-sacrificing deeds of endurance during the War Between the States.

The Women of the South in War Times

Turning the Other Cheek

As Sherman approached Atlanta during July of 1864, he sent Major General George Stoneman and a column of cavalry riding down the west bank of the Chattahoochee River. Sherman's orders directed Stoneman to cross the river and cut the railroad connecting Atlanta and West Point. This would not only disrupt a major Confederate supply line, but also divert attention from Major General Lovell Rousseau, who was leading another column of Sherman's horsemen on a destructive raid through central Alabama.

A brief clash with Confederate cavalry at Moore's Bridge kept Stoneman from crossing the Chattahoochee, and he soon began retracing his steps to rejoin Sherman. As his column leisurely rode northward, he sent out several detachments to scour the surrounding countryside, looking for horses, mules, and provisions.

One of these detachments, moving north on the main road between Carrollton and Villa Rica, stopped at the home of Preston H. Hesterly. Swinging down from their saddles, two Illinois soldiers approached the fifty-four-year-old farmer and told him they were going to take a matched pair of mules grazing in his pasture.

Hesterly protested he sympathized with the Union cause. He had voted against secession, he opposed the war, and he would be grateful if they would at least leave him one of those mules. But the soldiers told him several of their horses had been killed or crippled during the fight at Moore's Bridge, and Stoneman had ordered them to bring in every serviceable mount they could find.

With a sigh of resignation, Hesterly reluctantly led his unwelcome visitors into the pasture. As he came back to the house, he saw two or three more soldiers taking his gray mule, saddle, and harness. Others were emptying his smokehouse and ransacking his home.

"There was an officer about," Hesterly recalled. "He ordered them not to break up my things, told them not to pillage. He told the men to wait, that I would open the door for them. He said his men would not take anything they did not need."

But these Yankees seemed to need everything. During the next two hours, they relieved Hesterly of his silver watch and shotgun, all his knives and forks, as well as a large assortment of tinware and clothing, fifty pounds of tobacco, and two quarts of castor oil.

Then the raiders remounted and rode on, leaving Hesterly to pick up the broken pieces of his life. There were crops that needed harvesting, and he spent the next few days cutting a four-acre field of oats and tying them into large bundles. He had fifty dozen sheaves curing in the sun when, late on July 21, another swarm of blue-coated cavalrymen suddenly filled the road in front of his house.

They were the advance guard of General Rousseau's column, on their way to join Sherman after destroying twenty-six miles of railroad between West Point and Montgomery. A Yankee officer directed the first troopers into the field, where they dismounted and began hoisting the heavy bundles of oats across their saddles. Others rounded up about a dozen of Hesterly's chickens and took his cooking utensils and several sacks of corn.

"They seemed to be in rather a hurry," Hesterly noted dourly.

On July 22, Rousseau's raiders entered Sherman's lines near Atlanta, completing a 450-mile sweep through the heart of the Confederacy. Four days later, many of them were back in the saddle, riding south with Brigadier General Edward McCook in another attempt to cut the vital railroads that kept Atlanta fed.

Confederate cavalry caught up with McCook near Newnan, Georgia, on July 30, and cut his column to pieces at the battle of Brown's Mill. The raiders fled toward the Chattahoochee River, but their hurried retreat quickly became a rout that left hundreds of Yankee horse soldiers on foot. Desperately trying to avoid being captured and sent to Andersonville, they broke into small groups and scattered into the woods, hoping to reach the safety of Sherman's lines.

Among the fugitives were Captain Erastus G. McNeely of the 5th Iowa Cavalry and six enlisted men. Hiding by day and dodging Rebel patrols at night, they finally came to a familiar stretch of road, the same one they had traveled a few days earlier with General Rousseau.

That evening, Preston Hesterly heard a knock at his door. He swung it open and saw seven frightened, exhausted Yankee soldiers, begging for something to eat.

Hesterly had not forgotten what had happened two weeks earlier, when Stoneman's troopers took his mules and ransacked his house. Then Rousseau's men had taken most of what little was left. Hesterly had every right to be angry. He had every right to take his measure of revenge on anyone who wore a blue uniform.

But when these seven strangers appeared on his doorstep, asking for help, Preston Hesterly did not turn them away. Instead, he took them in and fed them. At the risk of his own life, he hid them from roving bands of Rebel cavalry, and then hired a man to guide them back to the Union lines.

Before McNeely and his companions left, they gave Hesterly a small piece of paper with their names signed beneath these hastily scrawled words:

If any of our troops Pass this mans house at any time Protect him for he is a good union man he fed and helped some of Genl McCooks Command that where dismounted.

Hesterly did not ask for a reward for what he had done. He did not seek any special favors. But after the war, he did file a claim requesting compensation for the three mules, the silver watch, and the other property he had lost. The United States government awarded him $402.00.

Compiled from P. H. Hesterly,
Southern Claims Commission Case Number 6,560,
Records of the General Accounting Office

Pity on a Prisoner

In the summer of 1863 Captain Harry Hunt, of Buffalo, New York, captain of a coasting vessel running out of New York City, married Miss Janie Scadden, daughter of Thomas L. Scadden, of Chicago, Illinois. After the wedding Captain Hunt took a number of his invited guests to New York and went aboard his vessel for a little pleasure trip at sea.

They had been out only a few hours when a United States revenue cutter ran across them and forced Captain Hunt to go down on the coast of North Carolina for a load of corn. While loading, Johnny Reb ran in on him and captured the vessel, wedding party and all; but after finding out that the party was composed of noncombatants, all were turned loose except Captain Hunt. His wife, thinking he would be released in a few days, refused to leave him; but instead he was finally sent to Andersonville Prison and both were held as prisoners of war.

In July 1864, I was ordered on duty at Andersonville to take charge of the dispensary and to superintend the building of a hospital and other government buildings connected with the prison. On the night of my arrival, I heard a very small infant crying near my office, which was in the "Star Fort" just outside the southwest corner of the prison. Upon inquiry, one of the guards informed me that it was the infant of Captain Hunt and his wife, only three days old.

Next morning I went down to see Mrs. Hunt and infant and found her in a tent in the most abject poverty I had ever seen.

While she was inside of the prison one night, the Federal prisoners cut the back of the tent that had been furnished her and Captain Hunt and stole her trunk, with nearly all of her clothes and some $5,000 in greenbacks that was in the trunk. She had been in prison thirteen months when her baby was born, and all she had to dress it in were some little wrappers that she had made out of an old calico dress, and her own clothing was hardly sufficient to cover her. I found on talking to her that she was a cultured, very intelligent woman.

I went back to my office and drew up a petition to General John H. Winder (who was in charge of the post) and got all of the surgeons at the post to sign it to have her boarded out in the neighborhood as soon as she was able to go. I presented the petition to General Winder, and he asked me what it meant. When I explained, he said he had forgotten that there was a lady prisoner there, but it would be against the rules of war to board her out, though he would like to do so if he could. I remarked to him that ofttimes things came up in this world that we had to shut our eyes to. He turned his face toward me, shut his eyes closely, and said, "Doctor, I don't see anything at all."

I left him and went out about a mile and a half from the prison to old Farmer Smith. He would not consider it at first, but finally told me to get the consent of his wife, and it would be all right with him if I would make it all right with the Confederate authorities. This I agreed to do and I then told Mrs. Smith what I wanted. She also refused, but I finally secured her consent.

That evening I went by train to Macon, Georgia, and asked a friend of mine, who was merchandising when the war broke out, for some goods to make clothing for a lady and her baby in prison at Andersonville. We went to his store and found a lot of remnants of flannels, calico, domestic, etc., enough to relieve her necessities until the war released her. When I got back to the prison I sent the goods to Mrs. Hunt.

I had Captain Hunt paroled when I first went there and appointed him a ward master in the hospital, so he could be with his wife. After they found out that I sent the goods, Mrs. Hunt wrote me the most beautiful and touching letter I ever read and with it sent a beautiful diamond scarf pin that Captain Hunt had worn for several years, which she begged me to wear as long as I lived. I wrote in reply that in her impoverished condition I could not and would not accept it. Two days after that Captain Hunt came to my office and told me that little Harry was very sick, and they wanted me to go to the house to see him at once. I said, "O, no, Captain, you can't fool me. You are only wanting me to go to the house so Mrs. Hunt can persuade me to wear the pin, and I am not going to do it." But finally I took the pin, because I could not reconcile Captain and Mrs. Hunt otherwise. . . .

W. J. W. Kerr,
Hospital Steward, Andersonville Prison
Confederate Veteran

At the Battle of Mobile Bay

The Confederate ram *Tennessee* started out from behind the fort just before the head of the line of Union warships was abreast of it, . . . but, receiving two or three broadsides, changed her course and ran back again, closely followed by the monitor *Tecumseh*.

As the latter neared the fort, pounding away at the ram with 15-inch solid shot, she struck a floating cask torpedo and exploded it. As was afterward ascertained by the divers, the explosion tore a hole in her bottom more than twenty feet square, and she sank like a stone—turning over as she went down in eight fathoms of water.

By this frightful disaster 110 out of 120 men were lost in a single instant. Commander Tunis A. M. Craven, one of the most gallant officers in the service, lost his life through his noble disregard of self. He was in the pilothouse with the pilot, close to the only opening in the whole ship, and this was only large enough to allow one man to pass at once. Craven was already partly out, when the pilot grasped him by the leg and cried, "Let me get out first, Captain, for God's sake; I have five little children!

Craven drew back, saying, "Go on, sir," gave him his place and went down with his ship, while the pilot was saved.

Assistant Surgeon William F. Hutchinson,
USS Lackawanna
MOLLUS Papers

Born in Battle

It was the summer of 1864, and the army under Sherman had fallen back from its position before Atlanta and swept around the rear of the city, General John "Black Jack" Logan leading the advance. I remember that the country was densely wooded, and that magnificent forests of pine, oak, and chestnut towered on either side of the road over which we marched. We were not molested until we neared the Flint River. There the enemy had planted a masked battery, and, as we approached, it enfiladed our line. You could scarce encounter more disagreeable travelers on a lonely road than shot and shell, and the boys were not long in taking to the shelter of the timber.

But General Logan at once ordered up a field battery of . . . "Napoleons," and presently accepted this challenge to an artillery duel. There was nothing to direct the fire of our gunners save the white puffs of smoke that could be seen rising above the foliage and the course of the enemy's shots; but they nevertheless soon silenced the Rebel cannon, and once more cleared the way for the column.

We then rode forward again, the writer in company with Dr. John M. Woodworth, the medical inspector of General Logan's staff. . . . Just as we turned a bend in the road, we emerged suddenly into a small clearing. A rude log cabin, surrounded by evergreen shrubbery, stood in the clearing, and hanging from one of the bushes we noticed a yellow cloth.

As medical officers, it naturally occurred to us at once that this was an improvised hospital of some sort, and we rode up to inquire. At the door of the cabin, as we approached, an old woman, evidently of the familiar "cracker" type, presented herself, but, on seeing that we were "Yankees," beat a hasty retreat. But we were not disposed to be so easily baffled and, calling her out again, began to ply her with questions.

She told us "there wa'n't no wounded men thar," and when asked why she had put out a yellow flag there, she replied, "Waal, yer see, my gal is sick, and I reckoned ef I put out that yer hosp't'l rag, you'ns wouldn't be pesterin' round so much."

"What's the matter with your child?" said I; "we are medical officers, and perhaps we can do something for her."

"Waal, now," she quietly responded, "ef you'ns is real doctors, just look in and see what you'ns all done with your shellin'. Time my gal was sickest, two of yourn shells come clar through my cabin, and, I tell you, it was right skeery for a spell."

We accepted the old woman's invitation and walked in. It was as she had said. The cabin, built of rough pine logs, afforded but one room, about twelve feet square. A small log meat house (empty) was the only outbuilding,—the cow stable having been knocked to pieces by our shells,—except a small bark-thatched "lean-to," at the rear of which we found a loom of the most primitive sort and constructed in the roughest fashion, containing a partially completed web of course cotton "homespun." Aside from this loom, the only household articles visible were an old skillet, a rather dilapidated bed, two or three chairs without backs, and a queer collection of gourds. The shells had indeed played havoc with the interior. The roof had been badly shattered, and a stray shot had pierced the walls. It had cut one of the logs in two, and forced one jagged end out into the room so that it hung threateningly over the bed upon which, to our astonishment, we saw lying a young girl, by whose side was a new-born babe with the prints of the Creator's fingers fresh upon it.

It was a strange yet touching spectacle. Here, in this lonely cabin, stripped by lawless stragglers of both armies of food and clothing, and shattered by the flying shells of our artillery, in the storm and fury of the battle had been born this sweet innocent. The mother, we learned, was the wife of a Confederate soldier whose blood had stained the "sacred soil" of Virginia but a few months after his marriage and conscription into service, and the child was fatherless. The babe was still clad in its own innocence, but the writer with his handy jackknife cut from the unfinished web in the old loom a piece of coarse homespun, in which it was soon deftly swaddled. Fortunately we had our hospital knapsacks with us, and our orderlies carried a little brandy, with a few medicines and a can of beef extract, and we at once did all that our limited stores permitted to relieve the wants of the young mother and child.

But by this time quite a number of officers, attracted by the sight of the yellow flag and our horses waiting at the door, had gathered about the cabin, and while we were inside, they amused themselves by listening to the old lady's account of this stirring incident. One of the officers had given her some "store terbacker," with which she had filled a cob pipe, and the fact that she was spitting through her teeth with such accuracy as to hit a fly at ten paces, nine times out of ten, showed that she was enjoying herself after the true "cracker" style.

Presently someone suggested that the baby ought to be christened with full military honors, and it being duly explained to her that to "christen" was all the same as to "baptize," she replied, with alacrity, "Oh, yes! baptized, I reckon, if you'ns has got any preacher along."

This was all the boys wanted, and an orderly was at once sent back to the general commanding, with the compliments of the surgeon and a request that a chaplain belonging to one of the regiments in the advance might be allowed to return with the messenger to the cabin.

The general asked the orderly for what purpose a chaplain was wanted, and the orderly replied that the doctors (mentioning our names) were going to have a baptism.

Upon this, General Logan (for he it was) significantly remarked that the names mentioned were in themselves sufficient to satisfy him that some deviltry was on hand, but that the chaplain might go. Then, inviting the colonel, who happened to be riding with him at the time, he set out himself for the scene, spurring "Old John" to a gallop, and soon had joined the party at the cabin.

"General," said the doctor, as the former dismounted, "you are just the man we're after."

"For what?"

"For a godfather," replied the doctor.

"Godfather to what?" demanded the general.

The matter was explained to him, and, as the doctor led the way into the house, the boys who had gathered around the general in expectation that the event would furnish an occasion for a display of his characteristic humor, noticed there was something in Black Jack's face that they were not wont to see there, and that in his eyes there was a certain humid tenderness far different from their usual flashing brightness. He stood for a moment silent, gazing at the unhappy mother and fatherless child, and their pitiful surroundings, and then, turning to those about him, said tersely, "That looks damn rough."

Then, glancing around at the ruins wrought by our shells and addressing the men in the cabin, he called out, "I say, boys, can't you straighten this up a little? Fix up that roof. There are plenty of 'stakes' around that old stable—and push back that log into place, and help the old lady to clear out the litter, and—I don't think it would hurt you any to leave a part of your rations!"

General John A. Logan

Prompt to heed the suggestion, the boys leaned their muskets against the logs, and, while some of them cut brush, others swept up the splinters and pine knots that the shot and shell had strewn over the floor, and not one of them forgot to go to the corner of the cabin and empty his haversack! It made a pile of commissary stores, consisting of meat, coffee, sugar, hardtack, and chickens (probably foraged from her next door neighbor), surpassing any that this poor "cracker" woman had probably ever seen or possessed at one time.

This done, the next thing in order was the christening, and the chaplain came forward to perform his scared office.

"What are you going to give her for a name? I want suthin' right peart, now," said grandmother.

She was told that the name should be satisfactory, and forthwith she brought out the baptismal bowl—which on this occasion consisted of a gourd—full of water fresh from the spring.

General Logan now took the baby, wrapped in its swaddling clothes of coarse homespun, and held it while the chaplain went through with the ceremony. The latter was brief and characterized with due solemnity, the spectators behaving with becoming reverence, and thus the battle-born babe was christened "Shell Anna. . . ."

The party now turned to leave the cabin and resume the march, when General Logan, taking a gold coin from his pocket—a coin that he had carried as a pocket-piece for many a day—presented it to the old lady as a "christening gift" for his godchild, and the officers and men, as they had recently drawn their pay, added one by one a "greenback," until the sum was swelled to an amount greater than this brave-hearted "cracker" had ever handled. Before parting, the general cautioned her to put the money in a safe place, lest some "damn bummer should steal it, in spite of everything," and then, ordering a guard to be kept over her cabin until the last straggler had passed by, he rode away. The old lady's good-bye was, "Waal! Them thar Yanks is the beatenist critters I ever seen!"

A Member of the 15th Corps
Washington Bulletin,
Quoted by the *Pittsburgh Reveille*

Mrs. McPeek

It was on the first day of September 1864. Confederate General William Hardee had been sent to Jonesboro from Atlanta with 22,000 men to head off a formidable flank movement of the enemy which was aiming to cut the Macon & Western Railroad and thereby compel evacuation of the city of Atlanta. The flank movement consisted of 40,000 or 45,000 men, and was commanded by General Sherman. . . .

As the two armies confronted each other two miles to the north and northwest of Jonesboro, it so happened that the little house and farm of Mrs. Alley McPeek . . . was just behind the Union line of battle when the conflict opened. Having nowhere to go she was necessarily caught between the fire of the two contending lines of battle, which were at comparatively close range and doing fierce and deadly work. The house and home of this old lady was soon converted into a Federal hospital, and . . . her yard and premises were literally strewn with the dead and dying of both armies.

During the whole of this eventful day this good and brave woman, exposed as she was to the incessant shower of shot and shell from both sides, moved fearlessly about among the wounded and dying of both sides alike, and without making the slightest distinction. Finally night closed the scene with General Jefferson C. Davis' 14th Army Corps in possession of the ground, and when the morning dawned it found this grand old lady still at her post of duty, knowing, too, as he did, the fortunes, or rather misfortunes, of war had stripped her of the last vestige of property she had except her little tract of land which had been laid waste. Now it was that General Davis, learning of her suffering and destitute condition, sent her, under escort and arms, a large wagonload of provisions, and caused his adjutant general to write her as follows:

Head-Quarters 14th Army Corps,
Department of the Cumberland
Near Jonesboro, Ga. Sept. 6th, 1864.

Mrs. McPeek

Will you please accept the accompanying provisions (The best we have to give.) for Ten or Fifteen Days with the best wishes of Col. Von Schrader Asst. Inspector Genl. Of the 14th Army Corps and myself.

We regret exceedingly that the fortunes of War should have made you suffer in the way you have done and cannot but confess that our hearts were touched by your unobtrusive account of your Difficulties this afternoon. I wish we could repair all that has been done to you by both armies and restore the pocket book which was taken from your daughter.

Random Acts of Kindness

We desire to thank you for your Kindness, and that
of your family, to our wounded during the night of the
1st inst. May Heaven reward you for it.

Very Respectfully

Your Obt. Servt &c.
A. C. McClurg
Asst. Adjt. Genl. & Chief of Staff

Compiled from the *Atlanta Constitution,*
Quoted by *Southern Historical Society Papers*,
with additional information from
Alley McPeek,
Southern Claims Commission Case Number 1,028,
Records of the General Accounting Office

A Rebel Heroine

In September 1864, General Philip H. Sheridan had recently assumed command of a small army, operating in the Shenandoah Valley. The 6th Corps was encamped near Claremont, on the eastern side of the valley, some twenty miles south of Harper's Ferry and about five miles north of Berryville. Winchester lay to the southwest about fifteen miles distant, beyond the Opequan Creek, which separated Sheridan's outposts from those of Confederate General Jubal A. Early's army.

On the morning of September 13, General George W. Getty's division moved out to Opequan for a reconnaissance. The Vermont brigade had the advance, the 3rd and 4th Vermont being deployed in front as skirmishers. Sheridan and General Horatio G. Wright, the commander of the 6th Corps, accompanied the column. At ten o'clock the skirmishers reached the creek and crossed it at once, meeting the Rebel pickets, however, but a short distance up the hill beyond. Captain Andrew Cowan's New York battery, going into position on an elevation on the hither side of the little stream, opened fire, the general hoping thus to develop the position of the enemy in the vicinity, his strength, and other information of that nature. The battery could be plainly seen from the opposite side of the creek; the skirmishers who had crossed were showing an occasional puff of smoke from their rifles, while the rest of the division was massed in a wood a quarter of a mile behind the artillery. The grove was clean and the shade was dense;

the men were scattered in groups among the stacks of arms, chatting carelessly or playing simple games.

The enemy presently planted a heavier battery than Cowan's upon a hill on the opposite side of the creek and returned his fire. Their first few shells, being aimed at too high an elevation, passed over the guns at which they were directed, ploughing through and exploding among the troops of the brigade which lay concealed in the timber. Several were wounded, and the lines formed for removal to some other position; but it being noticed that the missiles began to fall short of us, we were soon convinced that our presence was unknown to the enemy, and in a few minutes the danger was over.

Among those who were wounded on this occasion was Lieutenant Henry E. Bedell, of the 11th Vermont. He was a man of splendid physique, muscular and athletic, over six feet high, about twenty-eight years of age, a farmer, married, and the father of three children. Prior to his enlistment he had been a selectman of the town of Westfield, near the Canadian line. An unexploded shell crashed through his left leg above the knee, leaving flesh at either side, and a most ghastly mass of mangled muscles, shattered bones, and gushing arteries in between. As he lay upon the ground he screamed continually, "Cord it! Cord it! Don't let me bleed to death!"

The first rude tourniquet which a friend attempted to apply broke under the twisting of a ramrod, and allowed the spirting stream again to flow. But when the compression was complete he became quiet under the perhaps imaginary impression of temporary security, allowing himself to be lifted upon a stretcher and borne away to the surgeons and their ambulances without a groan. A field operation was speedily performed.

The leg was amputated at the upper third, nearly to the hip, everything being done for the sufferer that science and personal regard could suggest and that the rude circumstances permitted. Still, there was very little hope. Though his natural vigor was in his favor, his very size and the muscular strength on which he had prided himself were against him, for it was computed that over sixty-four square inches of flesh were laid bare by the surgeon's knife—to form the flaps which were stitched together across the surface left exposed. And it was also found that his right hand had been seriously injured, the bones of three fingers and of the middle hand being fractured and comminuted. The operation already performed had been so severe that it was thought best not to attempt the treatment of the hand until it was seen whether or not he would rally from the shock of the wounds and the amputation of the limb.

We returned to our camp about nightfall. The journey was a terrible trial to the wounded man. An ambulance under most favorable circumstances is hardly a downy bed of ease, and the jolting this remnant of a man for miles across the country, over fences and walls half torn down, and across ditches partially filled with rails, reduced the chances of his life to hardly one in a thousand, his immediate death being expected every moment. But, sustained by stimulants and his indomitable courage, at last in the darkness he reached the army lines alive.

Fortunately, a house was accessible, and the use of a vacant room in its second story was obtained, where Bedell was placed on a tick hastily stuffed with straw and resting on the floor. And to the surprise of everyone, he survived the night. A hope of saving his life was awakened. On the second day after the skirmish the surgeons decided to attempt the rehabilitation of the shattered hand. A finger or two were removed, the broken bones were adjusted, and the patient rallied in good spirits from the second administration of chloroform and shock to the system.

But his struggle for life was only just begun. After a few days of such rest as his miserable pallet could afford, orders were received in preparation for the coming battle of Winchester, or, as called by Sheridan, the battle of the Opequan, that all sick and wounded should be at once removed to Harper's Ferry. Army wagons and ambulances were therefore loaded with the unfortunates, and an attempt was made to transport poor Bedell with the rest.

But although he had previously endured a rougher journey, it was while his wounds were partially benumbed, as wounds always are for the first few hours, the nerves seeming paralyzed with the very rudeness of the injury. Now the torn flesh had become inflamed and was having its revenge. At every motion of the ambulance he groaned fearfully, and it was soon apparent that to carry him far would cost him his life. He was returned to his straw utterly exhausted, all but expiring.

The army was to move at two o'clock the next morning, September 19. The surgeons were forced to decide at once what they would do with the dying man. In fact, but one course was open, he must be abandoned to his fate. True, we were to leave him to the north of us, but in the valley no attempt was ever made to cover the long line of our communications. Strong escorts guarded our supply trains, and for the rest the Confederate raider, John S. Mosby, had free swing. Moreover, though it was not known at the time, Martinsburg was henceforth to be our base, instead of Harper's Ferry; and the vicinity of Berryville, where we then were, instead of being threaded once in four days or oftener by our caravans, as expected, was not revisited by our troops or trains for months. The wounded officer was therefore left on his chamber floor with a soldier nurse and such hospital stores as he would be likely to need for the next few days.

We fought the battles of Opequan and Fisher's Hill, "whirling" the enemy up the valley a hundred miles, for a month supposing the lieutenant dead. The attendant left with him followed us immediately; Bedell himself thought it best, and it was doubtless necessary, for the country swarmed with guerillas, and the system of bloody reprisals engaged in by Mosby and General George Custer reduced the probable life or death of the nurse to a simple question of time had he remained.

It appears that the family who allowed our officer the use of the naked room as a place in which to die were hardly pleased with their guest. In fact, they seem to have been utterly destitute of sympathy and to have thought it best for all concerned that he should leave the world, and them, as speedily as possible—and they left him at perfect liberty to do so. They were only a shiftless pair, who had temporarily taken possession of the basement story of the unoccupied farmhouse, the upper floors of which had been used as a field hospital by our surgeons. The promises they solemnly made to give the wounded officer care and attention were entirely neglected, and his chamber was never entered. Death, horrible in its loneliness and pain, would inevitably have come quickly had not a Good Samaritan appeared. A rebel among Rebels, there was a woman who proved herself to unite with a tender heart the rarest courage and perseverance beyond account.

Mrs. Bettie Van Metre was a Virginian, born in Luray Valley, gentle, graceful, and attractive, and less than nineteen years of age at the time in question. Her maiden name was Elizabeth Keyser. She had been educated in comfortable circumstances, and before the war her husband had been moderately wealthy, but now his farm was as barren as a desert, not a fence was to be seen, and there was nothing to protect, had any enclosure remained. There was a mill upon the premises, but the miller had gone to fight for his country, as he believed, and there was no grain left in the country to be ground. Officers who had called at her door remarked on the

Mrs. Bettie Van Metre

brave attempt at cheerfulness, which so manifestly struggled with her sorrow, and treated her grief with deference. For this delicately nurtured girl was living alone in the midst of war; battles had raged around her very dwelling; she was entirely at the mercy of those whom she had been taught to believe were her deadly enemies, and who held her husband and brother prisoners of war, taken while fighting in the Confederate army, the brother being, until long after this time, supposed to be dead. Her only white companion was a little girl, perhaps ten years of age, her niece. . . .

Through the gossip of the colored people in the neighborhood, Mrs. Van Metre learned that a Union officer was dying of wounds and neglect, perhaps half a mile distant from her home; and no sooner had she made the discovery than all her womanly sympathy was aroused. As she would have longed to have her husband or her brother treated under similar circumstances, so she at once resolved to treat their foe. She would not be moved by the sneers and taunts which were sure to come, but she would have him at her own house and save him if she could.

The lieutenant had now been entirely neglected for two or three days. He had resigned himself to death when this brave-hearted girl entered his chamber and with kindly and encouraging words called back his spirit from the mouth of the grave. The physician of the neighborhood, a kind old gentleman, Dr. Osborne by name, was soon summoned from a distance of several miles, and uniting personal sympathy with professional zeal, and with the universally philanthropic instincts of the old school country doctor, he promised his daily attendance upon the invalid. The chance was still but a slender one, so much had been endured, and so little vigor remained, yet those two good people determined to expend their most earnest endeavors in an almost desperate attempt to save the life of an enemy.

Mrs. Van Metre had been allowed to keep an apology for a horse, so old and broken-winded and rheumatic that he was not worth stealing, and also a rickety wagon. With the assistance of the doctor and a neighbor known as Uncle Dick, whose color permitted him to be humane, she carried the sufferer to her house and installed him in her own room. At last he found himself in a clean and comfortable bed, his wounds washed and his bandages cleansed; best of all, his wants anticipated by a womanly tenderness that inspired him with sweet thoughts of home.

The details of convalescence are always uninteresting. It is enough to say that Bedell lay for many days wrestling with death. At last he began to mend, and from that time his improvement was rapid. But although Mrs. Van Metre and the good doctor were able to supply the lieutenant's most pressing wants, still, much more than they could furnish was needed for the comfort of the invalid, and even for the proper treatment and dressing of his wounds. No stimulants could be obtained except the vilest applejack, and the necessity for them seemed absolute. No clothing was to be had, and he was still in his bloody garments. Delicate food was needed, but the impoverished Virginia larder had none but what was simple and coarse.

At Harper's Ferry, however, there was a depot of our Sanitary Commission, and stores in abundance. Someone must undertake a journey thither. It was a long day's ride to make the distance and return, and success was by no means assured even if the storehouse could be reached. It was in the charge of strangers. The lieutenant was too feeble to write, and even if he had been able to do so, there was no method of authenticating his signature. But a woman would be far more likely to succeed than a man, and, in fact, no man would be allowed to pass within the limits of the garrison encircling Harper's Ferry. So it came about that the feeble Rosinante, and the rattling wagon, and the solitary driver made the dangerous journey and brought back a feast of good things for the sufferer.

The picket had been beguiled by her eloquence to send her to headquarters, under charge of a guard which watched her carefully as a probable spy. The general in command had seen fit to allow her to carry away such trifling articles as the commission people would be willing to give; and although the chances were even that the gifts would be used in building up some wounded Rebel, still, the earnestness and the apparent truthfulness of her entreaty for relief overbore all scruples. The old-fashioned vehicle was loaded with the wished-for supplies, and the suspicious guard escorted the cargo beyond the lines.

The trip was repeated week by week, and when letters were received in answer to those deposited by the fair messenger, postmarked among the Green Mountains, her triumph was complete, and her draft good for anything the sanitary treasury contained. The only lingering doubt was in regard to the enormous amount of whiskey which the invalid required. Mrs. Van Metre, however, explained that it was needed for diplomatic as well as medicinal purposes. In that region, now abandoned to Mosby and his men, concealment was essential. Of course, it had been bruited about among the neighbors that the miller's young wife was nursing a Federal officer. Therefore, the old men who had heard of the convalescent must be taken into confidence and pledged to secrecy, a course rendered possible only by the liberal use of spiritus frumenti. Under the influence of such liquor as had not been guzzled in the valley since the peaceful days of President Buchanan, the venerable rascals were easily convinced that so shattered a life as that of the one-legged lieutenant could not greatly injure their beloved Confederacy.

On October 18, five weeks after Bedell received his wounds, General Sheridan was in Winchester, returning from Washington, and our army was encamped twenty miles away on the banks of Cedar Creek. The lieutenant greatly needed his valise from our baggage wagons. Therefore, a journey up the valley was planned, which at nightfall brought our heroine and her little niece to the headquarters of the 6th Corps, with a few words traced by the maimed right hand of her charge as her credentials.

Our feelings of wonder and admiration were most intense, as we learned from her simple story that our favorite who was dead was alive again, and felt how much true heroism her modest words concealed. It was plain that she had totally abandoned herself for weeks to the care of a suffering enemy, and yet she did not seem to realize that she deserved any credit for so doing, or that every woman would not have done as much. We loaded her with the rude attentions of the camp, and she spent the night comfortably (from a military point of view) in a vacant tent at General Getty's headquarters. The desired valise was then at Winchester, where she obtained it on her return.

The next daybreak found us fighting the famous battle of Cedar Creek. Amid the mounting in hot haste and the confusion of the morning's surprise, General Getty found time to commit his terrified guests to the care of an orderly, who by a circuitous route conducted them safely out of the battle. . . .

We heard nothing further from the lieutenant for several months. We eventually learned, however, that after a long period of careful nursing, varied only by the weekly errand of Mrs. Van Metre to Harper's Ferry for letters and supplies, the prudent doctor gave his consent that Bedell should attempt the journey home. Armed now with a pair of sanitary crutches, he doubted not that he could make his way, if he once could reach the Union lines. But the difficulty of getting to Harper's Ferry cost him much anxiety. Though at various times forty guerillas together had been in and about the house where he lay, the watchful care of his protector had thus far kept them in ignorance of his presence. This journey, however, was likely to prove much more difficult to manage.

At length one of the toddy-drinking neighbors, while relating his trials and losses, chanced to mention the seizure by our troops of a pair of his mules months before, and the fact that a Negro had since seen them in the Martinsburg corral. A happy thought struck the lieutenant; he at once assured the old gentleman that if he could only be placed (what there was left of him) in safety at the Ferry, the mules should be returned. The promise might perhaps be considered rash, seeing that Martinsburg was twenty-five miles from Harper's Ferry, under a different commander, that it was very decidedly unusual to restore property seized from the enemy for government use, that the chattels were probably long ago far up the valley with the army and especially that Bedell could not have, in any event, the faintest shadow of authority in the premises. But the old man jumped at the offer, and the bargain was struck.

It was decided that Mrs. Van Metre should accompany the lieutenant to Vermont, both for his sake, as he was yet months from recovery, and for her own, as she had now lived for years in unwonted destitution and anxiety, while a quiet, comfortable home was henceforth assured to her by her grateful charge until the return of peace; and who knew if she might not in some way regain her own husband, as she had restored another's.

So the party was made up and the journey commenced. The officer was carefully hidden in a capacious farm wagon, under an immense heap of straw. Two marauding parties were met during the day, but the cheerful smile of the well-known jolly farmer disarmed suspicion. The escape was successful. The clumsy vehicle drew up before headquarters at Harper's Ferry, and Bedell, saluted once more by a sentinel as he doffed his hat to the flag he had suffered for, headed the procession to the general's room.

The unique party told its own story. The tall lieutenant, emaciated, staggering on his unaccustomed crutches; the shrinking woman, timid in the presence of authority though so brave in presence of death; and the old Virginian aghast at finding himself actually in the lion's den, but the burden of an anxious longing written on his wrinkled face—each character so speaking—the group needed only this simple introduction: "General, this man has brought me in, and wants his mules."

General John D. Stevenson, warm-hearted and sympathetic, knowing somewhat of the previous facts, was able to comprehend the situation at once. He made the party sit down before him and tell him all their story. He fed them at his table and lodged them at his quarters. He applied for a special leave of absence for an officer and secured free transportation to Washington for both the lieutenant and the good woman who had saved his life; and finally, most surprising of all possible good fortune, he sent the venerable charioteer to Martinsburg, the happy bearer of a message that secured the restoration of his long-eared quadrupeds.

General Stevenson evidently forwarded to the War Department a somewhat detailed account of the transaction as known to him, including a suggestion that the husband of Mrs. Van Metre be released from his confinement as a prisoner of war. The following letter was received by return mail . . . :

Washington City, D. C.
November 4, 1864

Mrs. Van Metre,
Harper's Ferry.

Madam:

It is with the unfeigned pleasure that I comply with the instructions of the Secretary of War and inform you that he has ordered the unconditional discharge of your husband, now at Fort Delaware.

Mr. Stanton has been sensibly touched by the report received through General Stevenson of your noble and humane conduct towards a wounded Federal officer and soldier, and without a moment's delay has acted upon the suggestion of General Stevenson and ordered the discharge of your husband, as some acknowledgment of the feminine goodness and nobility manifested in your person.

If such an example could but extensively find imitations, it would do infinite honor to your sex, and greatly relieve war of some of its most barbarous tendencies.

Very respectfully your obt. servant,

E. A. Hitchcock,
Maj.-Gen. Vols.

1864

After several days of recuperation at Harper's Ferry, the lieutenant and Mrs. Van Metre went on by rail to Washington, where, of course, everyone treated them kindly and gave them all possible assistance. It came about that the quasi-widow and the crippled officer called together, by request, upon Secretary Stanton. That busiest of all busy men found time to hear the story, and despite the "stony heart" attributed to him by his enemies, he was deeply affected by the touching tale. . . . Tears rolled down his cheeks as he gave the formal order required for Van Metre's discharge from Fort Delaware, earned by acts that few women would have undertaken; and the couple, with glad hearts, crossing the street to the office of the commissary general of prisoners, presented the document to the clerk in charge to be recorded and vised.

But here another difficulty arose. On searching the records of the office, the name given in the order for discharge could not be found. The cruel report was made that no such prisoner had been taken to Fort Delaware. It was afterwards learned that after Van Metre's first capture he had escaped from Camp Chase in Ohio, had rejoined his command, and had been retaken at Spotsylvania, when he gave a fictitious name, fearing trouble if found fighting without a regular exchange.

Nevertheless, Mrs. Van Metre's information of his confinement at that place had been positive and her conviction of some mistake was sure. They laid the case before General Ethan Allen Hitchcock, then in charge of all prisoners of war, and again the story and argument was enough. With trembling hands the old gentleman endorsed the order: "The commanding officer at Fort Delaware will release any person the bearer may claim as her husband!"

The prison barracks were quickly reached. The commandant caused the thousands of grizzly captives to be paraded. File after file was anxiously, oh, how anxiously, scanned by the trembling

241

woman, and when the circuit was almost completed, when her sinking heart was almost persuaded that death instead of capture had been the fate of the one she loved, she recognized his face despite his unkempt hair and his tattered garments, and fell upon the neck of her husband as he stood in the weary ranks.

A few days more and both reunited families were at rest in Bedell's New England home, and the war, for them, was over. . . .

Major Aldace F. Walker,
11th Vermont Infantry
MOLLUS Papers

An Incident of a Sword

The battle of Jones Farm, about four miles south of Petersburg, Virginia, near the crossing of Boydton Plank Road and Church Road, occurred on September 30, 1864, and the day after, October 1st, it was decided that the advanced works near the Pegram house must be carried. Two battalions of sharpshooters were selected to do the work—one from General James H. Lane's North Carolina brigade and one from General Samuel McGowan's South Carolina brigade. It was thought desperate, and we were promised that the survivors would get thirty days' furlough.

We formed the two battalions in closed ranks and rushed on the works, carried them, and captured 240 prisoners. Our loss was so small that we did not get the thirty days' furlough. I had the honor of commanding Company A, Battalion of Sharpshooters, of McGowan's South Carolina brigade. . . .

We captured a young lieutenant, and I took his sword. I held him, as I could not spare a man to carry him to the rear. He reminded me it was against the usages of war to keep a prisoner under fire, but at that time every man was needed, and I had rather have let him go than lose a man. In a few minutes, I saw prisoners being carried to the rear and I turned the lieutenant over to them. My sword being rough (Confederate make), I put it aside and donned the lieutenant's.

The next day we had a truce to bury the dead. I went out to superintend and met a Federal officer. I noticed he was scrutinizing my sword, and he asked me if I "would part with it." I told him it was a trophy and could not be bought.

He said, "Pardon me, I did not mean to offend you; but that sword belonged to an officer killed in front of Petersburg, and I had it in keeping to return to his widow. I loaned it to a young officer until he could get one from the North, and I would give anything to recover it."

I unclasped it from my belt and handed it to him, saying, "I present it to the deceased officer's wife."

He thanked me and took it. He then asked me to give him a safeguard to bury some of his dead on the left of my line (his right). I told him I would go with him. After burying the dead, he told me to come inside of his line in the rear of his rifle-pits, and we walked until I got opposite the center of my line. He again thanked me and said, "If the fortune of war ever throws you in my hands, I will remember this." I bowed and returned to my lines.

Some time after, my sergeant came to me and said there was a flag of truce coming in front. I told him to meet it, and he returned with a handsome sword (made in Newark, New Jersey), saying the officer begged me to accept it. I have regretted ever since that I did not ask his name. He should have sent his card, but I suppose in the hurry he forgot it. I still have the sword and value it beyond price. I am sure this is the first instance of an officer presenting a sword to his enemy. . . .

Lieutenant Nathaniel Ingraham Hasell,
1st South Carolina Infantry
Confederate Veteran

1864

Caring for a Wounded Enemy

I was a lieutenant and assistant quartermaster of the 9th Tennessee (Union) Cavalry, and was present and participated in the battle of Morristown, Tennessee, October 28, 1864, between the Federal forces commanded by General Alvan C. Gillem, consisting of his brigade, composed of the 8th, 9th, and 13th Tennessee (Union) Cavalry, and Battery E, 1st Tennessee (Union) Light Artillery; and the Confederate forces consisting of General John C. Vaughn's brigade and the 16th Georgia Battalion of Cavalry. . . .

The forces were about equal. The battle did not last a great while, but more gallantry was never displayed on any battlefield of the war. The Federal troops charged and captured 5 pieces of artillery, 224 prisoners, including 19 officers, and the Confederates left 85 dead on the field, including 6 officers.

The battle closed at night, and no soldier who ever went over a field of that kind will forget the groans and pleading for water. We held the field and were hunting for our own wounded with torches and gathering up at the same time the Confederate wounded, taking them to the same field hospital, where our surgeon treated them as they did our own.

The frost was in the air. I remained until my duties called me to ride across the field, and I overheard some loud talking in a clump of bushes and rode up to see what it was. I found two Federal soldiers standing over a wounded soldier cursing him and threatening to kill him, as they said he was a spy and had on a

"Yankee overcoat." The man on the ground wounded was a Confederate soldier and protested that he had picked up the overcoat in a skirmish and was no spy. The battle had been one in which we lost not a great many, but those lost were favorites, and our men were mad.

I ordered the two who were standing over the wounded man not to kill him, but to go back to their commands if they couldn't help take care of the wounded without butchering them. The wounded soldier was shivering from the cold, as his "Yankee overcoat" had been taken from him, and I took my blanket from under my saddle and wrapped it around the wounded man and asked him what was his name. He gave me the name of Gid T. Smith, of . . . the 43rd Tennessee (Confederate) Infantry. He said he belonged to a company that was raised in Meigs County, Tennessee, where I was born and raised.

Humanity demanded that I put this poor fellow where he could get the service of a surgeon and where he wouldn't freeze to death. It was late, and the only men of our command who had seen this man I had driven off. About this time I heard approach what I knew from the noise on the frozen ground (for it was night) was a body of cavalry. I knew that if I made myself known and they were Confederates I should probably be made a prisoner. I knew also that I couldn't move the man myself, and if he couldn't get relief at once he would die. I took the risk, hailed the approaching column, made myself known, and, as it turned out, the command was a part of my own regiment, commanded by Captain D. M. Nelson.

I made known the facts, Captain Nelson made a detail and sent back to our camp for an ambulance, and we gathered together some wood, built a fire and remained with this wounded "Johnny Reb" until the ambulance came and took the wounded man back to the hospital.

I ascertained that the wounded man had been shot through the lower part of the bowels, the ball passing through him, and that he was a son of Captain Jack Smith, an old and honored citizen who resided near Decatur, in Meigs County, Tennessee. I wrote to his father, whom I knew well, and he came to Knoxville and nursed his boy to health.

That wounded soldier is now the postmaster at Census Post Office, Meigs County, Tennessee, and has been partly paralyzed from that wound since the night of October 28, 1864. He has as fine a wife and family of children as can be found in the state of Tennessee.

I am an old man now, and write this simply as matters of that kind ought not be lost. All of us know that "war is hell," but many such acts occurred which should not be lost to history. . . .

Lieutenant E. H. Matthews,
9th Tennessee (Union) Cavalry
Confederate Veteran

Only a Private

Louis Abear was a private in Company H, 5th Michigan Cavalry, and made a good soldier. At the battle of Trevilian Station he was taken prisoner, and before his release he was confined in five different prison pens and town jails.

While he was in Millen Prison, in Georgia, an exchange of sixty prisoners was to be made. The officer of the day told off sixty names at the door of the pen, but for some reason, probably because he was too ill, or perhaps dead, one man did not come forth. At that moment, Louis, who had been sent out after fuel, under guard of course, came through the gates pushing a wheelbarrow loaded with wood.

"Here. Louis, here's a chance for you. We want sixty men to go north and are short one. Jump into ranks here!" exclaimed the officer.

"To be exchanged?" asked Louis, trembling more than he did when under fire.

"Yes, be quick."

"Then take Hank. He's sick and will die if he remains here," and Louis darted into the hospital ward.

Hank had a pair of pantaloons and shoes, but no coat or hat. Louis pulled off his, put them on Hank, and brought him out, weak and tottering. As Hank filed out of the gate and once more breathed the air of freedom, Louis, hatless and coatless, took hold of the handle of his wheelbarrow and started for another load of wood.

Can mortal mind conceive of such an act? It cost him seven months of a living death, and all for a man with whom he was not intimately acquainted.

And now the other side of the picture. Ever since the close of the war, until a few months ago, when Hank died, these two men have lived right here in Wayne County, Hank with a home and family, Louis with neither. They have met occasionally, but at no time did Hank ever refer to the act in Millen Prison that set him free and saved his life; never invited him to his home; never alluded to the past or addressed his savior other than a mere acquaintance. On his deathbed, however, he told the story, and asked his relatives, if they ever had an opportunity, to befriend Louis, for his sake. It was tardy acknowledgement of one of the noblest acts the world has ever known.

Detroit Free Press,
Quoted by *Southern Bivouac*

On the March to the Sea

But a few days out of Atlanta, in a sandy, poverty-stricken region, . . . we found in a small log cabin two wee girls, one about three, the other five years old, the only living objects about the place. In the cabin were a few rude housekeeping articles, a bed in one corner that would not tempt a soldier out of a horse stable as a sleeping place, and a bake kettle, a few gourds, and a homemade "piggin" were about all to forage on. The little ones, so nearly dead of starvation and neglect, could tell us nothing, only "mamma gone, mamma gone." Clothed in nothing but thin cotton dresses, black with dirt and grease, no underclothing, their little bare legs and arms so grimed with dirt that at first we thought them "darkies."

The little cotton dresses were but bags with a hole left for the arms and neck. They were as shy as young partridges, but food soon won their confidence. A search was made all about the premises for other living beings, but the little ones were absolutely alone, but for the birds that chirped about in the treetops nearby.

The command halted to feed and rest their animals. A fire was built on the hearth, and the babies given a bath with warm water and fed on soldiers' grub. Their tangled flaxen hair was combed and, well washed, they were as pretty a capture as ever made by the "Bummers Bold."

Resuming our march, we tried to give them away at the next cabin a few miles on our route, but that would not work—the woman had a house full of her own. She knew nothing about these two, and so half a dozen places were visited, but with war's devastation in the country none could be found to care for our motherless girls.

But before night the bummers had a wardrobe for them worthy of the command. A piece here and there as the cabins were passed, were borrowed. Before the night camp was reached, a soldier who had babies of his own in Michigan removed the dirty cotton gowns and clothed them in the plunder of the afternoon; "they were just too sweet for anything." They were mounted on a pack mule that day; at night they slept cuddled up in a soldier's arms. The rain dripped down through the pine trees, drenching the blankets of the tentless soldier, but the little ones were as comfortable as "bugs in a rug."

Those two sisters were turned over to the regiment next day; by turns they were toted on the backs of the soldiers to Savannah. The authorities of the city were notified, but nobody had time for "the little white trash." A lieutenant, wounded and sick, was granted a furlough; he took them home to the state where they reside today in happy homes, beautiful in their motherhood. Although diligent search was made after the war, the mystery was never solved. They are simply two of "Sherman's bummers."

Captain Charles E. Belknap,
21st Michigan Infantry
MOLLUS Papers

Two Unknown Heroes

At the time of General Hood's defeat before Nashville, the brigade to which my regiment belonged . . . was detached and operating with General N. B. Forrest in the vicinity of Murfreesboro. Hood's retreat in the direction of Columbia placed the enemy on the direct line between our little force and the main body of the army, and in consequence we were obliged to make a wide detour by a forced march across the country to regain our place in our division line. In this march the men suffered terribly, as large numbers of them were barefooted and there were not half a dozen overcoats in the brigade, while the weather was intensely cold and the whole earth covered with sleet and snow. We reached Columbia at about nine o'clock at night, at least the head of the column did; but "the lame and the halt" were coming up by ones and twos all night.

Early the next morning we were formed to march through the town, the 1st Georgia in the lead. In the first file of fours was a young fellow of about twenty years, who on the march of the day before had been compelled by physical weakness to throw away a part of his burden as a soldier. He had parted with his blanket and held on to his musket. Now, as we marched, with indomitable pluck he was at the head of the regiment, though his trousers were worn to the fringe from the knees down and his bare feet, cracked and bleeding, left their marks upon the frozen road. At this moment a private of cavalry came riding by—he turned and looked at the poor lad—then reining in his horse he threw his leg over the pommel of the saddle and took off first one shoe and then the other; and throwing the pair of them down at the poor fellow's feet with these words, "Friend, you need them more than I do," he galloped away. . . .

Colonel Charles H. Olmstead,
1st Volunteer Georgia Infantry
Southern Historical Society Papers

"Let Me Show You"

It occurred in the fall of 1864. At that time I was a first lieutenant of engineers and one of the four officers assigned for special duties to the staff of the chief engineer of the Army of Northern Virginia, Brigadier General Walter H. Stevens. Our quarters were near the Osborne Turnpike, about four miles below Richmond.

I had just returned to camp from a long, hard day's duty. The weather was drizzly, and I was thoroughly chilled. There were only a few coals and smoldering chunks where the fire had been. The servants were all away, and our camp seemed deserted.

Dismounting and hitching my horse, I gathered some wood and small sticks, raked the coals together and began to make a fire. While on my knees, vigorously blowing the coals to ignite the kindling, I heard someone ride up and dismount. I felt so forlorn and was so intent on my undertaking that I did not look up to see who it was. In a few moments he walked up to where I was and stopped at my side. Still I did not look up. Imagine my surprise when, in a gentle and sympathetic voice, which I recognized at once, came the words, "My boy, let me show you how to make that fire."

It was General Robert E. Lee. I arose instantly, saluted, and attempted an apology. Then, stooping down with me, General Lee pulled the wood open at the top and told me to take the coals and kindling from off the ground underneath and lay them in the opening.

"This is the way," he said, "the old servants showed me how to make a fire when I was a boy;" and then he explained the philosophy of it. In a short time we had a roaring fire, which we enjoyed alone until the other officers returned to camp.

That young engineer cherishes to this day the fact that the commander of all the Confederate armies assisted him in making a fire. The desolation of the place was transformed more by the genial presence of General Lee than can be imagined.

Lieutenant William A. Obenchain,
Engineers, Army of Northern Virginia
Confederate Veteran

"Mother, Don't You Worry"

One day an old countrywoman, footsore and travel-stained with walking all the way down from New Jersey, arrived in Washington and made her way to the White House. She inquired for the president and was told by his private secretary to take a seat—he was engaged just then. And so she sat down and waited all day, while others came and went (diplomats, army officers, etc.), but at last she was admitted to Mr. Lincoln.

"Well," he said kindly, "mother, what can I do for you?"

"Oh," she replied, "Mr. Lincoln you can do a great deal for me. My son, John, is a soldier in the 7th New Jersey and they are going to shoot him, and I want you to save him."

"Why, how is that? What has he been doing? What are they going to shoot him for?"

"Why, you see, it is this way. His regiment went on a long march—marched all day and part of the night—and when they halted, the rest of them lay down and went to sleep. But John and some others were put on guard as sentinels, and John walked his beat for a while, but got tired and sat down for a little rest and fell asleep; and while he was sleeping the officer of the day came along and found him, and they arrested him and put him in the guardhouse, and court-martialed him, and ordered him to be shot, and it is not right, and I want you to save him. John has always been a good boy. His father was killed on the Peninsula. His brother died in a hospital. And John is all I have left. And he is a good boy—sends

256

nearly all his pay home—helps with my rent and grocer bills—and I am getting old and can't work as I used to—and now if they shoot John, I shall starve and have to go to the poorhouse, and that is not right. Now won't you please help me save John? Our member of Congress has been down here, but Mr. Stanton would not see him and said John must be punished. And so I have come down here myself—walked all the way from New Jersey to see what you would do for me."

"But don't you know he has been guilty of a grave offence—'sleeping on post'—a very grave military offence? He was put there to safeguard the army. Suppose General Lee and his army had come up just there, and found John asleep, and got inside our lines; they might have surprised General Meade and our army and worked great havoc."

"Yes, but General Lee and his Rebels didn't come up, and didn't surprise Meade and our boys, and there wasn't any havoc, and so I don't see why they should now shoot poor John. He didn't do any harm. He is a good boy, and he didn't mean to go asleep. And now, Mr. Lincoln, O won't you pardon him?"

"No, my good woman, I can't do just that. What would Stanton and Meade say? But I will telegraph General Meade to suspend his sentence, and that will be all right."

"No, Mr. Lincoln, that won't do. General Meade might not get it, and you might forget, and they would shoot John after all."

"Oh, mother, don't you worry about that. General Meade will get it today, and I shall not forget—I am not built that way. If the facts be as you say, they won't shoot John until I order him shot. And if they don't shoot him until I order him shot, he will live to be an old man! And besides, the war will soon be over now, and the soldiers will go 'Marching home' and John along with them."

"Say, clerk," turning to one of his executive clerks, "send this old lady down to the Soldiers' Home near the New York Station, and ask them, in my name, to give her supper, and lodging, and breakfast, and tomorrow morning get her a pass over the railroad to New Jersey, wherever she wants to go."

And then turning to the old woman he said very graciously, "There, mother, that is all I can do for you today, good-bye."

And so with a "God bless you" and streaming eyes she bade Mr. Lincoln "good-bye," and the great president saved the life of another Union soldier.

Captain James F. Rusling,
Assistant Quartermaster, U.S. Volunteers
MOLLUS Papers

1865

MALICE TOWARD NONE

Random Acts of Kindness

How I Lost and Recovered My Hat

Every old soldier of the Army of Northern Virginia remembers the campaign from the Wilderness to Petersburg, when Lee outgeneraled Grant at every point and, despite Grant's overwhelming numbers and resources, won from him a series of splendid victories. And we all remember our life in the trenches, when, with starvation rations and an inadequate supply of clothing, less than 40,000 men had to guard forty miles of breastworks and be constantly on the alert against a foe more than four times our numbers and abundantly supplied with rations, clothing, and everything necessary to the efficiency of an army.

The opposing lines were so close together at some places that the penalty of any exposure of the person was death or severe wounds. I remember going one day to the lines just south of the Appomattox River to visit my old company (D, 13th Virginia Regiment), in which I had had the honor of serving the first year. The lines were so close together that loud talking in one line could be easily heard in the other.

There were in the breastworks immense beams with portholes for the muskets, and iron shutters to protect them when no firing was going on. I was looking through one of these portholes at "our friends, the enemy," fearing that some particular bullet might strike in that particular hole at that particular time, when a sudden gust of wind lifted my hat and landed it in between the lines. It was a new blockade hat, for which I had invested some three hundred dollars; but I gave it up at once, as I would not have risked going after that hat for all the hats that ever ran the blockade.

I was on my way to the bombproof of a friend to borrow a second-hand hat—think of a second-hand Confederate hat in February 1865—when my old comrade, George Hauer, came up and said, "Chaplain, I'll get your hat."

His proposition to get my hat was earnestly declined, and I thought that I had dissuaded him from the undertaking, and had actually borrowed a second-hand hat and was about to leave the trenches, when the brave fellow came up with a proud smile and said, "Here is your hat, Chaplain."

"Why, how did you get it, George?"

"O, I crawled down the trench leading to the picket post and fished it with a pole."

"Did not the Yankees see and shoot at you?"

"Yes, they did," and the brave boy held up his right arm, with which he had worked the pole, and showed a number of bullet holes through the sleeve. He added, "I reckon they would have plugged me anyhow before I could get the hat, but I called out, 'Stop your foolishness, Yank. I am doing you no harm. I am just trying to get my chaplain's hat!' A good-natured fellow replied, 'All right, Johnny; I will not shoot again if you will hurry up and get it before the officer comes with the relief.'"

Chaplain John William Jones,
13th Virginia Infantry
Confederate Veteran

A Case of Mistaken Identity

I was a member of Company G, . . . 5th Regiment Georgia Cavalry, . . . General Joseph Wheeler's corps. After repulsing the enemy at Aiken, South Carolina, driving back their cavalry under General Judson Kilpatrick to their infantry column, which was heading for Columbia . . . , our cavalry took up a line of march parallel for the same point.

It was a very cold day and night, rain and sleet falling steadily on us as we marched in column en route—everything covered with ice, icicles hanging from our hat rims and stirrup guards. The manes, tails, and fetlocks of our horses were frozen, and a bridge we crossed had to be sanded continuously to enable our horses to keep their feet while mounting and descending the slopes at either end. It was some time after night before we halted and went into camp for the rest of the night.

We soon had big fires burning, and after drying our clothes and warming, we wrapped up in our blankets and lay down by the fires to get what rest and sleep we could. At dawn, we were up and by sunrise were again in our saddles and on the march.

Our regiment, the 5th Georgia, headed our column, and shortly after leaving our camping ground we were passing a field on our right enclosed with a rail fence which was about thirty feet from the road. On the fence were perched about two dozen soldier boys, wrapped in the regulation overcoats, enjoying the warm rays of the rising sun, which felt good after our experience of the day and night just preceding.

I will here state that the majority of our boys wore over their uniforms rubber "ponchos," or the United States overcoat of blue, involuntarily supplied by the boys in blue. The boys on the fence had left their arms at their camp, and, as was usual, chaffing began between them and the boys on the march; but all at once a discovery was made which caused the boys on the fence to fall off like so many cooters off a log in a mill pond and scoot like wild turkeys for the other side of the field. The discovery was mutual, but before any shots were fired at the fleeing Yanks some big-hearted Johnny among us called out in a loud voice, "Don't shoot them, boys; they haven't any arms; let them go."

The Yanks on reaching the other side of the field looked around at us; and, it appearing that no effort was being made by any of us to pursue them and no shots were fired at them, they stopped, waved their hats at us, and leisurely entered the woods beyond, rejoining their comrades. Evidently we had camped within a hundred yards or so of each other during the night under the impression that we were a part and parcel of the same command. . . .

Private James T. Lambright,
5th Georgia Cavalry
Confederate Veteran

With Sherman in South Carolina

On the march through Georgia to the sea, the devastation was not through any hatred of the section through which the army passed, but under the direction of corps commanders. It was more or less relentless according to the measure of local hostility manifested by the inhabitants.

In South Carolina, the same orders to respect the houses of private citizens were in force, but the soldiers knew that the state was the originator of secession and had led all her sister states into rebellion, and a revengeful feeling against her filled their hearts, or rather a joyful feeling over being able to pay an installment of a debt long overdue. . . .

The plantation houses—mostly deserted by their wealthy owners, who had fled in fear—were large and luxurious in their furnishings, but somehow they all seemed to have in them a tendency to ignition. One would see a fair mansion set on a hill and as he looked the smoke would begin to roll out its windows and from its rooftree, and presently only a pair of blackened chimneys remained to mark its site. . . .

Looking backward from this distance, I cannot remember that any of us felt any sadness at seeing the destruction of venerable or even historic homes that had sheltered Greene or Cornwallis or Tarleton, or that we were moved to any active measure to stay the waste. One day, however, when our brigade had the advance, an incident occurred that was an exception.

Random Acts of Kindness

I was riding on ahead of the column with another staff officer, as our custom was, for the purpose of getting to the camping ground before nightfall so as to look it over by daylight and be able to guide the regiments to their places, when I noticed a plantation house near the road, with all its buildings unharmed and its dooryard free from squads of foragers. As we came abreast of the place, a gentleman of middle age and of good bearing came hastily out to the road and besought me, with most appealing looks and words, to give him a guard for his property. I answered briefly, and probably coldly, that I had no guard to give him; that he would have to take his chances, etc. Upon that he renewed his entreaties more urgently and asked me who was the general in command and where he could find him, adding that he was sure any general would protect his library from destruction, at the same time waving his hand toward a detached, one-storied, frame building near the house. A separate library building twenty-five or more feet square on a remote plantation piqued my curiosity, and I asked him his name.

Every man who is old enough to remember the pleasure which in the 1850s *Richard Hurdis,* and *Border Beagles,* and their author's other border stories gave to reading boys will understand what a thrill of excitement and interest ran through my veins as my interlocutor answered with a bow, "William Gilmore Simms, Sir."

All my indifference vanished instantly, and his hope rose perceptibly as I told him of the joyful days and nights which the creations of his pen had brought me in my far away Wisconsin home. His heroes had been as real to me in my teens as are the great captains of the Wilderness and Atlanta to the youth of today, and I told him that I owed him a debt of gratitude which I would be glad to try to pay.

Very soon the head of the column came up, and I went at once to General Charles Ewing to report the reason of my delay on the road and to intercede for Mr. Simms and his library. On learning whose place it was and nature of the owner's request, the general ordered guards to be detailed and placed there, but to remain only until the brigade had passed and then to report to their regiment. The general then explained to Mr. Simms that he would have to seek a like favor from the next following brigade and so on until all had passed.

Having done what I could in return for the many happy hours given me years before, I bade Mr. Simms good-bye and rode rapidly on to make up for the time I had waited there. I confess I did not feel very sanguine that his books and buildings would escape unscathed, so when some years after the war I read that they were all burned I was not surprised, but I was sincerely grieved that they were so unfortunate as to be in the pathway of war.

Lieutenant Frank H. Putney,
12th Wisconsin Infantry
MOLLUS Papers

Who Is Thy Neighbor?

On my way home from Andersonville late in March 1865, we stopped at Jackson, Mississippi, where news reached us of the capture of the ambulance train sent out from Vicksburg. It was captured by bushwhackers, who killed the drivers, burned the ambulances, and escaped with the horses.

Dr. John C. Bates, C.S.A., who was in command, gave us the information and said if there were any who thought they were able to march the forty-four miles to Vicksburg in four days, he would provide a wagon with provisions and a guard, and we could get an early start the next morning.

About seventy-five undertook the journey. Twelve reached a blacksmith shop ten miles distant that evening. I was among that number. The driver of the wagon, being a young lad like myself, suggested that I "keep close to the back of the wagon," which permitted me to hang on to the tailboard with one hand, making the journey possible. We made the ten to eleven miles each day. On the third day the wagon left us to return to Jackson. As we approached a large swamp crossed by a well-worn corduroy road, I found it quite impossible to proceed, having to use a crutch, and I persuaded the "boys" who were with me to leave me at the roadside near a large tree and send back an ambulance for me when they reached our lines.

Soon after they had gone I heard the tramp of a horse and the old Southern song, "There's No Use Kicking Up a Row." Very soon the horseman was in hailing distance, and I called out, "Hallo, there, Johnny!"

Not seeing me, he stopped and looked around, and I called again. He then rode up to me. My legs were so badly swollen by the march and scurvy that I had been obliged to rip my pants, leaving my limbs at the mercy of the flies.

As he approached me he said, "Why, Yank, what are you doing here?"

I answered his question, concluding with, "I haven't got very much, but I'll give you all if you will let me ride your horse across the swamp."

He dismounted, saying, "What's the matter with you?"

I simply threw the old ragged pants off my legs, saying, "You can see for yourself."

He then said, "It would be a hardhearted man who would refuse you a ride. Give me your hand, Yank," and he helped me on his horse, saying, "Let old Boney have a free rein and he'll take you safely over the swamp, and I'll go over the logs and catch you there."

I frequently liken this incident to the "man on the road from Jerusalem to Jericho" and the Master's answer to the question, "Who is thy neighbor?" This young soldier was from Texas.

Corporal James M. Emery,
3rd Pennsylvania Heavy Artillery
Confederate Veteran

A Generous Enemy

I have thought more times than I can count of the kindness of a young Yankee soldier to me, a newly made prisoner, at General Grant's headquarters, near Dinwiddie Courthouse, on the night of April 1, 1865. I was a member of Company H, 5th North Carolina Cavalry, and in the forenoon of the day, being in momentary anticipation of a battle, we had fortified ourselves by broiling meat just sent us from home and eating it with quantities of hardtack we had drawn as rations.

At two in the afternoon, we took up our part in the battle of Five Forks, and in one of our dismounted charges we crossed a swollen stream, where many of us had to swim, and all were wet to our necks. In the varying fortunes of the day, our colonel and lieutenant colonel, with other officers and many men, were killed and many others were captured, I among them.

As the night came on, I was nearly freezing in my wet clothes, and at the same time was famishing for water. My thirst amounted to a craze. Every Yankee that came near me I begged for water, but not one paid me the slightest attention.

At ten o'clock we reached General Grant's headquarters, where we were to spend the night on the wet ground and with nothing to protect us from the cold. I was facing the prospect of a bitter night when the officer came to post the relief. My lips were quivering so with cold that I could scarcely form the words, but I begged again for a drink of water.

"Stand here," he said kindly, "until I post the relief." In a short time he came back, led me to his tent, gave me water, and bade me warm myself by his fire. He then began to talk to me, telling me of the sad plight of the Confederate army and saying that within three days Richmond would fall.

I could not agree with him, and began to paint in roseate colors the morale of the Confederate army, its courage and constancy, and the fortifications and defenses around Richmond and Petersburg, which had already proved themselves impregnable against Grant. But in my heart I knew he was right. The end was near. Yet somehow, though he had been kind to me, I did not want him to know that I had given up. Nor did I realize that the end would come as soon as it did. That was the 1st, and Lee surrendered on the 9th.

When he was ready to leave his tent, the young officer asked for my word as a soldier that I would not try to escape and then left me by his fire with his overcoat for a pillow and a sheepskin to lie on. He waked me at the first streak of day and walked with me back to the "bull ring," during which walk I gave him as a souvenir my wooden canteen, whose rarity he had admired, and he gave me in exchange his own canteen, and then pressed on me a good-sized greenback to help me through the hard days that might come. We parted like brothers, but neither thought of the other's name; and now, after nearly fifty years, I am still hoping to find him once more. If this should be seen by him or by any of the guard at General Grant's headquarters on the night of April 1, 1865, I hope it may be made known to me, that I may meet again my long-lost friend whose path and mine once crossed "as ships that pass in the night."

Private J. D. Hodges,
5th North Carolina Cavalry
Confederate Veteran

"That Was My Brother"

During the few eventful days which immediately preceded the fall of Richmond, Abraham Lincoln tarried at City Point, Virginia, awaiting the news from Grant, Meade, and Sheridan, who were pulverizing Lee's right wing. . . . Time hung wearily with the president, and as he walked through the hospitals or rode amid the tents, his rueful continence bore sad evidence of the anxiety and anguish which possessed him.

Presently, however, squads, and then hundreds, and later thousands of prisoners, of high and low degree, came from the front, and we all began to realize from what we saw of their condition, and what the prisoners themselves told us, that the Confederacy was crumbling to pieces.

Among the captured were Generals Richard S. Ewell, Custis Lee, and Rufus Barringer, who became the guests of myself and wife, I being at the time commander of post, and right well did they enjoy the only good square meals that had gladdened their eyes and their palates for many a long day.

General Barringer, of North Carolina, was the first to arrive. He was a polished, scholarly, and urbane gentleman, scrupulously regarding the parole I had exacted from him, and deeply sensible and appreciative of my poor efforts to make him comfortable.

Hearing that Mr. Lincoln was at City Point, the general one day begged me to give him an opportunity to see him as he walked or rode through the camp, and happening to spend that evening with the president in the tent of Colonel Theodore S. Bowers, Grant's adjutant general, who had remained behind to keep up communication with the armies operating across the James River, I incidentally referred to the request of General Barringer.

Mr. Lincoln immediately asked me to present his compliments to the general, and to say he would like very much to see him, whispering to me in his quaint and jocose way, "Do you know I have never seen a live Rebel general in full uniform?"

At once communicating the president's wish to General Barringer, I found that officer much embarrassed. He feared I had overstepped the bounds of propriety in mentioning his curiosity to see the Northern president, and that Mr. Lincoln would think him a very impertinent fellow, besides which he was muddy and tattered and torn and not at all presentable.

Reassuring him as best I could, he at last sought those embellishments which a whisk, a blacking brush, and a comb provided, and we walked over to headquarters, where we found the president in high feather, listening to the cheerful messages from Grant at the front.

I formally presented General Barringer, of North Carolina, to the president of the United States, and Mr. Lincoln extended his hand, warmly welcomed him and bade him be seated. There was, however, only one chair vacant when the president arose, and this the Southerner very politely declined to take.

This left the two men facing each other in the center of the tent, the tall form of Mr. Lincoln almost reaching the ridgepole as he slowly removed his eyeglasses, looking the general over from head to foot, and then in a slow, meditative and puzzled manner, inquired, "Barringer? Barringer? From North Carolina? Barringer, of North Carolina? General, were you ever in Congress?"

"No, Mr. Lincoln, I never was," replied the general.

"Well, I thought not; I thought my memory couldn't be so much at fault. But there was a Barringer in Congress with me, and from your state, too."

"That was my brother, sir," said Barringer.

Up to this moment the hard face of the president had that thoughtful, troubled expression with which those of us who knew him well were only too familiar, but now the lines melted away, and the eyes and the tongue both laughed. I cannot describe the change, though I still see it and shall never forget it. It was like a great sudden burst of sunshine in a rainstorm.

"Well! Well!" exclaimed the great and good man, burying for the moment all thought of war, its cares, its asperities, and the frightful labor it had imposed upon him, his heart welling up only to the joyous reminiscence which the meeting brought to him.

"Well! Well!" said he, "Do you know that that brother of yours was my chum in Congress. Yes, sir, we sat at the same desk, ate at the same table. He was a Whig and so was I. He was my chum, and I was very fond of him. And you are his brother, eh? Well! Well! Shake again."

And once more in the pressure of his great hand his heart went out to this man in arms against the government, simply because his brother had been his chum and was a good fellow.

A couple more chairs by this time had been added to the scant furniture of the adjutant general's tent, and the conversation drifted from Mr. Lincoln's anecdotes of the pleasant hours he and Barringer had spent together, to the war, thence to the merits of military and civil leaders, North and South, illustrated here and there by some appropriate story, entirely new, full of humor and sometimes of pathos.

Several times the general made a movement to depart, fearing he was availing himself too lavishly of Mr. Lincoln's affability, but each time he was ordered to keep his seat, the president remarking that they both were prisoners, and he hoped the general would take some pity upon him and help him to talk about the times when they were both their own masters and hadn't everybody criticizing and abusing them.

Finally, however, General Barringer arose and was bowing himself out, when Mr. Lincoln once more took him by the hand, almost affectionately placed another hand upon his shoulder, and inquired quite seriously, "Do you think I can be of any service to you?"

Not until we had all finished a hearty laugh at this quaint remark did the president realize the innocent simplicity of his inquiry, and when General Barringer was able to reply that "if anybody can be of service to a poor devil in my situation, I presume you are the man," Mr. Lincoln drew a blank card from his vest pocket, adjusted his glasses, turned up the wick of the lamp, and sat down at Colonel Bowers' desk with all the serious earnestness with which you would suppose he had attached his name to the Emancipation Proclamation.

This was, however, all assumed. He was equipping himself and preparing us for one of his little jokes. While writing, he kept up a running conversation with General Barringer (who was still standing and wondering) to this effect, "I suppose they will send you to Washington, and there I have no doubt they will put you in the Old Capitol Prison. I am told it isn't a nice sort of a place, and am afraid you won't find it a very comfortable tavern; but I have a powerful friend in Washington—he's the biggest man in the country—and I believe I have some influence with him when I don't ask too much. Now, I want you to send this card of introduction to him, and if he takes the notion he may put you on your parole, or let up on you that way or some other way. Anyhow, it's worthwhile trying."

And then very deliberately drying the card with the blotter, he held it up to the light and read it to us in about the following words:

> This is General Barringer, of the Southern army. He is the brother of a very dear friend of mine. Can you do anything to make his detention in Washington as comfortable as possible under the circumstances?
>
> A. Lincoln.
>
> To Hon. Edwin M. Stanton,
> Secretary of War

Barringer never uttered a word. I think he made an effort to say, "Thank you," or "God bless you," or something of that kind, but he was speechless. We both wheeled about and left the tent.

After walking a few yards, not hearing any footsteps near me, and fearing Barringer had lost his way, I turned back and found this gallant leader of brave men, who had won his stars in a score of battles . . . audibly sobbing and terribly overcome.

He took my arm, and as we walked slowly home he gave voice to as hearty expressions of love for the great Lincoln as have been since uttered by his most devoted and lifelong friends. . . .

Brigadier General Charles H. T. Collis
Quoted by *A Woman's War Record*

At Appomattox

General Lee said, "I suppose, General Grant, that the object of our present meeting is fully understood. I asked to see you to ascertain upon what terms you would receive the surrender of my army."

General Grant replied, "The terms I propose are those stated substantially in my letter of yesterday; that is, the officers and men surrendered to be paroled and disqualified from taking up arms again until properly exchanged, and all arms, ammunition, and supplies to be delivered up as captured property."

Lee nodded an assent and said, "Those are about the conditions which I expected would be proposed."

General Grant then continued, "Yes, I think our correspondence indicated pretty clearly the action that would be taken at our meeting, and I hope it may lead to a general suspension of hostilities and be the means of preventing any further loss of life."

Lee inclined his head as indicating his accord with this wish, and General Grant then went on to talk at some length in a very pleasant vein about the prospects of peace. Lee was evidently anxious to proceed to the formal work of the surrender, and he brought the subject up again by saying, "I presume, General Grant, we have both carefully considered the proper steps to be taken, and I would suggest that you commit to writing the terms you have proposed, so that they may be formally acted upon."

"Very well," replied Grant, "I will write them out." And calling for his manifold order book, he opened it, laid it on a small oval wooden table, which Colonel Ely S. Parker brought to him from the rear of the room, and proceeded to write the terms. The leaves had been so prepared that three impressions of the writing were made. He wrote very rapidly and did not pause until he had finished the sentence ending with "officers appointed by me to receive them." Then he looked toward Lee, and his eyes seemed

Lee and Grant at Appomattox

to be resting on the handsome sword that hung at that officer's side. He said afterward that this set him to thinking that it would be an unnecessary humiliation to require the officers to surrender their swords, and a great hardship to deprive them of their personal baggage and horses, and, after a short pause, he wrote the sentence: "This will not embrace the side-arms of the officers, nor their private horses or baggage."

When he had finished the letter, he called Colonel Parker to his side, and looked it over with him, and directed him as they went along to interline six or seven words, and to strike out the word "their," which had been repeated. When this had been done the general took the manifold writer in his right hand, extended his arm toward Lee, and started to rise from his chair to hand the book to him. As I was standing equally distant from them, with my back to the front window, I stepped forward, took the book, and passed it to General Lee. . . .

Lee pushed aside some books and two brass candlesticks which were on the table, then took the book and laid it down before him, while he drew from his pocket a pair of steel-rimmed spectacles, and wiped the glasses carefully with his handkerchief. He crossed his legs, adjusted the spectacles very slowly and deliberately, took up the draft of the terms, and proceeded to read them attentively. They consisted of two pages. When he reached the top line of the second page, he looked up and said to General Grant, "After the words 'until properly' the word 'exchanged' seems to be omitted. You doubtless intended to use that word."

"Why, yes," said Grant; "I thought I had put in the word 'exchanged.'"

"I presumed it had been omitted inadvertently," continued Lee, "and, with your permission, I will mark where it should be inserted."

"Certainly," Grant replied.

Lee felt in his pocket as if searching for a pencil, but he did not seem to be able to find one. Seeing this, I handed him my lead pencil. During the rest of the interview he kept twirling this pencil in his fingers and occasionally tapping the top of the table with it. When he handed it back, it was carefully treasured by me as a memento of the occasion.

When Lee came to the sentence about the officers' side arms, private horses, and baggage, he showed for the first time during the reading of the letter a slight change of countenance, and was evidently touched by this act of generosity. It was doubtless the condition mentioned to which he particularly alluded when he looked toward General Grant as he finished reading and said, with some degree of warmth in his manner, "This will have a very happy effect upon my army."

General Grant then said, "Unless you have some suggestion to make in regard to the form in which I have stated the terms, I will have a copy of the letter made in ink and sign it."

"There is one thing I should like to mention," Lee replied, after a short pause. "The cavalrymen and artillerists own their own horses in our army. Its organization in this respect differs from that of the United States. . . . I should like to understand whether these men will be permitted to retain their horses."

"You will find that the terms as written do not allow this," General Grant replied; "only the officers are permitted to take their private property."

Lee read over the second page of the letter again and then said, "No, I see the terms do not allow it; that is clear."

His face showed plainly that he was quite anxious to have this concession made, and Grant said very promptly, and without giving Lee time to make a direct request, "Well, the subject is quite new to me. Of course, I did not know that any private soldiers owned their animals, but I think we have fought the last battle of the war,—I sincerely hope so,—and that the surrender of this army will be followed soon by that of all the others; and I take it that most of the men in the ranks are small farmers, and as the country has been so raided by the two armies, it is doubtful whether they will be able to put in a crop to carry themselves and their families through the next winter without the aid of the horses they are now riding, and I will arrange it in this way: I will not change the terms as now written, but I will instruct the officers I shall appoint to receive the paroles to let all the men who claim to own a horse or mule take the animals home with them to work their little farms. . . ."

Lee now looked greatly relieved, and though anything but a demonstrative man, he gave every evidence of his appreciation of this concession, and said, "This will have the best possible effect upon the men. It will be very gratifying, and will do much toward conciliating our people."

> Colonel Horace Porter,
> General Ulysses S. Grant's staff
> *Campaigning with Grant*

Washington City on the Night of Mr. Lincoln's Assassination

Mr. Lincoln was assassinated by John Wilkes Booth in Ford's Theater in Washington City. The editor of the *Banner* was there— not in the theater, but in Washington City—and he will never, never forget it. He was not there by invitation of Mr. Lincoln or of any member of his cabinet, nor was he there in the capacity of a congressional lobbyist or office seeker.

He arrived in the city that evening (Friday, April 14) about three o'clock on a fine steamer from City Point—Grant's base of supplies on the James River. He didn't put up at the Ebbitt or take rooms at the Riggs House, but contented himself, as best he could, with a humble place on the floor of the old capitol. He and his accompanying friends, some three or four hundred in number, received a good deal of attention on their arrival in the famous and splendid city. At the wharf, he was met by a full regiment of handsomely uniformed soldiers with flags flying and a band playing national airs. He and his friends were not so well clad. Some had shoes and some had not; some had hats and some had not; some had coats or jackets and some had not; but all of them had a big appetite and a long face.

Washington was then enjoying a smile that covered its whole face. Everybody seemed to be gay and happy. Everybody, it seemed, had on his or her holiday attire—men, women, boys, girls, were all out on the streets, glad and rejoicing. Lee had surrendered.

The grand old Army of Northern Virginia, which, for four long, weary, terrible years of battle and blood, had stood as a stone wall between the Army of the Potomac and the Confederate capital, had gone down in defeat. The clouds of war, black and dismal, that had hung like a pall of death over the national capital for four years, were flying in all directions, and the sun of peace, full-orbed and cheery, was shining in glorious splendor. The great national heart was beating regularly and happily and sending healthy blood to the utmost limits of the national body, and brought in its backward flow tidings of gladness and joy from all parts of the great republic. Many and joyous were the congratulations given and received. The beardless boy, who had for years bivouacked on many a tentless field, threw his arms, in the ecstasy of his joy, around the neck of mother and brother and sister and wept what words could not tell; and father and mother and sister, in silence that spoke volumes of gratitude to Him who holds all in the hollow of His hand, hugged the boy to their throbbing bosom. Everybody was glad and happy, except the poor, dejected, ragged, footsore, and almost broken-hearted Confederate prisoner.

Yet he, as he tramped along the streets to the Old Capitol Prison, catching now and then a sight of the glad and joyous faces, and witnessing occasionally the happy embrace of mother and her returning boy, felt grateful that his life had been spared during the most terrible and bloodiest of civil wars. He sighed deeply as he looked upon these scenes and thought of the loved ones far away, and of the time when he, too, could step in the front door of his old home in the distant sunny South and receive the sad welcome that awaited him. But when he recalled the fact, as many a poor Confederate prisoner did, that his old home had been destroyed by the relentless waves of war, that the loved ones were gone he knew not whither, that one or more of his brothers and scores of his friends had fallen in the last heroic struggles around Petersburg and along the line of Lee's retreat, he bowed his head in silence and wept as he never wept before.

Who can tell how a Confederate prisoner felt on the streets of Washington City on April 14, 1865? Witnessing scenes of joy, hearing the shouts of final triumph, looking into faces that spoke a gladness that words could not express, no doubt, as he felt, the picture of despair.

Alas, what a dreadful, what a terrible blow was awaiting that vast congregation of happy people who crowded the streets of Washington on that ever-memorable day—April 14, 1865! The hand was raised which, that night at ten o'clock, was to strike a blow that would stagger the whole nation; that would cause a shriek of woe to be heard throughout Christendom; that would send sorrow and grief and mourning throughout the length and breadth of the land; that would awaken mingled feelings of sympathy and rage wherever civilization had left a footprint!

And the blow was given!

That night at ten o'clock, in the midst of a crowded theater, Mr. Lincoln was assassinated and, in his own home in the same city, Mr. Seward's throat was cut!

The news spread rapidly, not only over the city, but over the whole country. In the city, the shock must have been terrific. It is said that men staggered as if intoxicated, and women screamed when they heard it. It was late, after midnight, before the terrible deed became known among the masses of the people, but when it was known, they came out upon the streets, gathered upon the corners, discussed the situation, and the more they discussed it the more excited they became. The city was moved to its very depths, and it was evident that the mob spirit was uppermost.

Just at this juncture of affairs, someone recalled the fact that a large lot of Confederate prisoners had been brought in that evening and were confined in the old capitol. "Hang 'em," "shoot'em," "burn'em," became the cry, and to carry this threat into execution preparations were made. Ropes were procured, knots were made, everything ready for a general massacre of the helpless Confederate prisoners who knew nothing on earth of the occurrences of the night. Within the walls of the old capitol they were sleeping and dreaming of "home, sweet home," or perhaps of the last charge at Five Forks or Sailor's Creek.

At that time General Green Clay Smith . . . was a representative in Congress from Kentucky. He saw what was going on and witnessed the preparations being made to usher into eternity the helpless and innocent Confederates in the old capitol. Realizing what a terrible deed it would be for a mob to hang, shoot, or kill three or four hundred helpless men on the streets of Washington who were innocent of any complicity in the assassination of Mr. Lincoln, he procured the services of two or three friends to hold the mob in hand by speaking until he could see Secretary Stanton and provide some means, if possible, to protect the prisoners from the rage of the mob.

His friends—God bless them, whoever they were and wherever they are—responded promptly, mounted a box on the streets, and addressed the mob. When one had said all he could say, another followed him, and so on, occupying half an hour, perhaps an hour; thus giving General Smith time to see Mr. Stanton.

General Smith went, or rather ran, to . . . Mr. Stanton, . . . told him briefly of what was going on in the streets, and begged for troops to protect the unarmed prisoners from the mob. Mr. Stanton told him "to go and do as he thought best." General Smith left in a run, soon found a battalion of troops on the streets, took charge of them, rushed them to the old capitol, arriving just in time to place them between its walls and the enraged mob—just in time to save from a terrible death some three or four hundred helpless Confederate prisoners.

During the night the prisoners suspected that something

Green Clay Smith

unusual was going on, though they had not the slightest idea what it was. Guards were doubled, troops were marching, horses galloping all night, all of which they could hear. Next morning at daylight we were told by the guard that Mr. Lincoln had been shot in Ford's Theater and was dead; that Mr. Seward's throat had been cut and he was dying; that a mob was on hand to destroy us. We looked out through the windows and saw files of soldiers with fixed bayonets, artillery unlimbered in the streets and loaded, cavalry with drawn sabers, and a mob whose very look was appalling.

Our feelings can be imagined, but they cannot be described. The writer of this went in the gray light of the morning in the backyard to get some water at the pump, but he could not drink. He tried to wash his face and hands, but he could not. He sat down upon an old trough, placed his head in his hands, and sat there absorbed in thought until a friend touched him on the shoulder and asked him what was the matter.

The mob lingered about the prison several hours before it broke. Its dispersion lifted a load from the bosoms of the prisoners that had weighed them down to the very ground. On the Sunday following, the prisoners left for Johnson's Island, Lake Erie, where they were kept until grim-visaged war had smoothed its wrinkled front in all parts of the Confederate States.

To General Green Clay Smith, then a representative in Congress from Kentucky, Temperance candidate for president in 1876, at present pastor of the Baptist Church in Mt. Sterling, Kentucky, and a gentleman of the noblest impulses and finest nature, the Confederate prisoners in the old capitol at Washington on April 14, 1865, are indebted for their lives. But for his exertions they would have suffered the most horrible of deaths—death by hanging, shooting, burning by an infuriated mob. There were not a thousand men in Washington that night who would have done as General Smith did! May God bless him and his all through time and eternity!

> Captain Cornelius Tacitus Allen,
> Lunenburg (Virginia) Artillery
> *Princeton* (Ky.) *Banner*
> Quoted by *Southern Bivouac*

Lincoln's Legacy

The conflict in Missouri was a bitter, personal, and revengeful one. I remember, the day before President Lincoln's assassination, a lady came to see me whose son was about to be executed for murder committed as a guerrilla. She had been to Washington to save him and had seen the president. She brought me Mr. Lincoln's card, on the back of which he had written:

> My Dear General Dodge:—Cannot you do some-
> thing for this lady, who is in so much trouble?

I understood the case: that, while he would not interfere, he hoped that I could see my way to do so, and he disposed of the lady in that way.

The lady, in presenting the case, supposed that card alone would pardon her son, but when I told her I would consider it, she was indignant and left, no doubt determined to report me to the president and appeal over my head.

That evening President Lincoln was assassinated; all officers holding important commands were notified in the night, so that they could prepare for the excitement that was bound to come. The lady called the next day and asked me for the card; said she desired to keep it as a memento, no doubt giving up all hope for her son; but I did not have it in my heart, after Lincoln's death, to carry out the order of the court, and therefore commuted the sentence to imprisonment.

Major General Grenville M. Dodge
MOLLUS Papers

Random Acts of Kindness

1865 & Beyond

WHEN THE ROLL IS
CALLED UP YONDER

Random Acts of Kindness

How a Confederate Got Home in 1865

My experience in getting home from Greensboro, North Carolina, to Hardeman County, Tennessee, will perhaps serve to show that there were some big-hearted men serving in the Yankee army.

I belonged to Company E of the 12th Tennessee Infantry, with which the 22nd and 47th Tennessee Regiments were consolidated. I was paroled on May 1, 1865, near Greensboro, North Carolina. During the negotiations between Generals Johnston and Sherman, I "picked up" a very good-looking mule and all the feed I could for him, picturing in my fancy a nice time riding that mule home; but the morning I was to start, someone stole my mule, so I walked to an uncle's, sixty or seventy miles away.

I learned from men who had belonged to Lee's army that the Federal government was issuing transportation and rations to paroled soldiers. My uncle carried me back within easy reach of Greensboro, where I would take the train to go home. There I found "Billy Yanks" every way I looked. Going to the headquarters of the commanding general, I asked for the transportation and rations to paroled soldiers, but was told that they had orders from Washington not to issue any more.

I was nearly a thousand miles from home, seventy miles from an acquaintance, and penniless. Walking aimlessly along, I noticed two Yankee soldiers on the street whom I sought to avoid, feeling that I could expect no comfort from them under existing conditions.

In passing, one of them hailed me as "Johnny Reb," and I walked up to him. He asked me where I lived, and I told him near Memphis, Tennessee. Then, reminding me that I was a long way from home, he asked if I had money. After telling him of my condition and inability to get any transportation home, he remarked to his comrade, "I'll be damned if that is right." He then asked as to my command and remarked that we "were good ones"—that his command had confronted us, and he could testify that we didn't do all the running. He then asked, "Johnny, what are you going to do?" and I expressed my utter loss to know what to do.

"Well, Johnny," he said, "let me tell you what I'll do. My regiment, the 26th Kentucky Federal, has orders to leave here tomorrow or next day for Louisville, Kentucky, to be mustered out of service. Go with me to my camp, and I'll divide my grub and anything else you'll need till we get there."

I thanked him and took his name, regiment and company, and where he was camped, as I hadn't made up my mind whether to accept or not, knowing that there were always some insolent men in a camp, and that I would be at the mercy of the entire regiment. He called my attention to the blue blouse he had on and said that he would dispose of any impositions on me.

I sauntered around until near sundown, when I concluded to look up the regiment and my strange new friend. I found it about three-quarters of a mile from town, and going to the tents, asked an officer for the company designated. He inquired if I had an acquaintance in the company and then wanted to know how long I had known him. I said two or three hours, when he remarked, "Very short acquaintance."

I walked down the row of tents and found my new and untried friend. The big-hearted man threw the tent flap back and said, "Come in, Johnny Reb, and make yourself at home." Night soon came on, and he divided his supper with me and provided a place for me to sleep, and next morning the same way.

That day or the next the regiment took a chartered train, my friend telling me to get on with him. We hadn't gone far before the conductor discovered me in gray mixed up with the blue. He asked if I belonged to that regiment, and of course I said I did not, when he said that the train was for that regiment and I would have to get off. I couldn't object, of course, but my new friend came to my rescue, telling the conductor he had asked me to come and go as far as Louisville with him, that he was dividing his rations with me, and that if I were put off he could be put off, too. The conductor passed on, and I was never bothered any more.

For some reason, we had to stop over a day or so near Weldon, North Carolina, where we camped in the pine woods. My friend, Jim Sands, suggested to the company one day that another pile be made from the company's rations, so that "Johnny Reb" could have some. This was agreed to, and the company commissary sergeant made an equal division, including me.

They had telegraphed to Baltimore for a meal to be prepared for the regiment. After landing, they marched in order along the streets. I went to the sidewalks, but kept in sight of the regiment. The women of Baltimore were the strongest (if possible) Southern women I ever met. They soon filled my haversack with the best. As the regiment was filing into a large building, my friend called me to come in and get a place. As I wanted some coffee, I took a place near my friend and told him I had grub enough for us both to Louisville. He said he was glad I had found some friends.

We took the Baltimore and Ohio Railroad through the Alleghenies' beautiful scenery, and at Pittsburgh we took a steamboat down the Ohio River, arriving in Louisville without a hitch, except dragging over a sand bar once.

Random Acts of Kindness

At Louisville we marched to the barracks, and the next day I told my friend I would go down into Louisville and see if I could find anyone acquainted with my people from whom I could get money to go home. He said that if I couldn't find anyone to come back and stay with him until they were mustered out and paid off, when he would let me have money to go home on.

While in Louisville, one merchant gave me a dollar. I noticed that a Mississippi steamer was to leave for Memphis and New Orleans at 2:00 p.m. that day; so I went on the vessel, introduced myself to the captain, and told him I wanted to go to Memphis with him, that I had been in General Johnston's army, had no money, and didn't know any one there, and that I had a parole from General Sherman. He made some inquiries as to my home and acquaintances, then told me to go and register and the clerk would show me a berth. I was seven days and nights on the steamer *St. Francis* in July 1865, and it was delightful traveling. The captain of the boat was named Hart. When he came in sight of the high bluff at Memphis, I told him to step up the bluff to a large building I pointed out and I would go get him his money (I had never inquired what it was). He told me to go on; that it was all right.

I got home July 15, 1865, the day after the burial of my youngest sister, knowing nothing of her death until I got home.

I was wounded eight times during that terrible war. Some of the very best friends I have had since were in the smoke of battle against us. I wrote to my Yankee friend, James Sands, at Ironton, Ohio, several times. The moral courage he showed under the circumstances demonstrated the true brotherhood of man as I had never known before.

Private John T. Bowden,
12th Tennessee Infantry
Confederate Veteran

A Moment's Contemplation

While Jefferson Davis was being sent to Fortress Monroe, he was tried by a mock court, "the court" being made by a number of officers on board the United States steamer *Pontoosuc*, then acting as guard of the transport *Clyde*, who determined to avenge the assassination of Mr. Lincoln by the execution of Mr. Davis.

Ensign J. J. Kane, a noted marksman . . . was selected to fire the fatal shot. The other passengers on the *Clyde*, besides Mr. Davis, were his wife, sister, and three children, Vice-President Alexander H. Stephens, Postmaster General John H. Reagan, Senator Clement C. Clay and wife, General Joseph Wheeler and staff, Colonels William Preston Johnson and Francis R. Lubbock of Davis' staff, Major Victor Maurin, Captain George V. Moody, Lieutenant Leland Hathaway, and several privates.

The event as reported by Kane is substantially as follows:

"Mr. Davis was sitting in a steamer chair on the deck of the *Clyde*. It was a clear day, and I could see him as plainly as if he had been but one hundred feet away. I loaded an Enfield rifle I had picked up on the battlefield of Fort Fisher, and resting the muzzle in an air port, aimed it at the heart of Davis. I feel confident I could have sent a bullet to the target, but some influence prevented me from pulling the trigger.

"'I can't do it,' I said to my comrades, but they urged me to fire, and said I would be justified in doing so. 'It would be murder,'

I said, and one of them answered, 'Think of the death of Lincoln.' With that I took aim again and even touched the trigger, but a psychological force I now think was of divine origin prevented me from doing the act which would have ruined me forever after.

"I still hesitated, however, and was still aiming when the little daughter of Davis came on deck with a lady who was probably her mother, and ran into her father's arms. It was then impossible to shoot without endangering the life of the little girl, and I laid up the gun. A short time afterward, and before the child had left the arms of its father, the vessels drifted apart, making it impossible for any of the other officers to do the killing.

"I have been thankful ever since that I was restrained from doing what would have been an extremely rash act, and I have never until now related the incident except with a requirement of secrecy."

Confederate Veteran

How Grant Saved Lee

The war was over. General Lee and his Confederates had returned to their desolated homes on their parole of honor. The victorious armies, under Grant and Sherman, were encamped around Washington, and Jeff Davis was in Fortress Monroe.

Generals Grant and Rawlins were playing a game of billiards in the National Hotel, and two civilians were indulging in that pastime on an opposite table. A major entered the room in a hurry and whispered to Grant. The latter laid his cue on the table, saying, "Rawlins, don't disturb the balls until I return," and hurried out.

One of the civilians said to the other, "Pay for the game and hurry out. There is something up."

In front of the hotel stood a mounted sentinel. Grant ordered the soldier to dismount and, springing into the saddle, rode up the avenue so fast as to attract attention. The first civilian questioned the soldier as to the cause, but received no answer. On being told of the general's breakneck ride, it was decided to go to the War Department and learn the cause.

One of the civilians came, asking me if I knew the reason of General Grant's hasty action and if I had seen the hero of the hour around the department. I answered, "Yes," but was surprised at anybody's knowledge of the event. When told of what had transpired, I said, "Well, as you are aware of the coming of General Grant, I will tell you about it, providing you promise not to repeat it."

Secretary Stanton had sent for me in reference to the execution of certain orders, and, while listening to his instructions, General Grant came in. The secretary greeted the general with a pleasant "good morning," which the latter returned and said, "Mr. Secretary, I understand that you have issued orders for the arrest of General Lee and others, and I desire to know if such orders have been placed in the hands of officers for execution."

"I have issued writs for the arrest of all the prominent Rebels, and officers will be dispatched on the mission soon," replied the secretary.

General Grant appeared cool, though laboring under mental excitement, and quickly said, "Mr. Secretary, when General Lee surrendered to me at Appomattox, I gave him my word of honor that neither he nor any of his followers would be disturbed so long as they obeyed their parole of honor. I have learned nothing to cause me to believe that any of my late adversaries have broken their promises, and I have come here to make you aware of that fact, and to suggest that your orders be canceled."

Secretary Stanton became terribly angry and said, "General Grant, are you aware whom you are talking to? I am the Secretary of War."

Quick as a flash Grant answered back, "And I am General Grant. Issue those orders at your peril."

Then, turning on his heel, Grant walked out as unconcerned as if nothing had happened.

Neither Lee nor any of his soldiers were arrested. I was dismissed from the presence of the secretary with the remark that my services in connection with the arrest of the leading Rebels would be dispensed with until he took time to consider, and I yet await the result of his decision.

Captain Franklin H. Barroll,
Provost Marshal General's Bureau
Camp-Fire Sketches and Battle-Field Echoes

I Had Been Her Slave

My old master, William Wynn, . . . enlisted in the 8th Georgia Regiment, State Guards, . . . Company D. He took me as his body servant, and after the war everything was lost to him—even myself came near being lost to him, but not quite.

After the war, he moved to Prescott, Arkansas, and began farming; but he was quite old and feeble, so he could do but little at it. Later, he wrote me that he could get a pension under the Arkansas laws, but he was too feeble mentally and physically, and he wanted me to do it for him.

I replied that I would do anything in my power on earth for him and his wife, as long as they lived. I went at once to . . . the ordinary for Bibb County, Georgia, got application blanks, took one to every member of the old company that I could find, got them signed with affidavits before proper officers, made oath myself, and had seals put on where seals could be found. Sad, but true, he died just before I got the papers ready.

I then went back and got other blanks, and did the same work for his widow. I paid every cent of money necessary without any cost to her. I sent all the papers for him and her both, and the committee put her on the pension list. She wrote me her sincere thanks for what I did, and said she was all the more grateful because I had been one of her slaves.

Jerry W. May,
Confederate Veteran

Amos Rucker, Negro Veteran

There is an underlying note of tenderness in every heart, and it vibrates to the touch of real pathos, as a violin does to its bow. The story of Amos Rucker, the old Negro veteran of Atlanta, carries its own moral. Amos belonged to the Rucker family of Colbert County, Georgia, belonged in a wider sense than as a mere human chattel that the slaves were said to be, for every joy or sorrow in "ole Marster's" family touched its sympathetic chord in his heart. The children he watched grow up were as dear to him as his own, and "ole Miss" was always the pinnacle of all that was good in his eyes.

Amos was a young man at the time of the war, and when "Marse Sandy Rucker" went to the front, Amos went too, just as proud as was that young soldier of his "marster's" gray uniform and brass buttons.

In all those long, hard years the 33rd Georgia Regiment bore its part in the bloody struggle, and there was no braver member than Sandy Rucker, and shoulder to shoulder with him fought Amos, as though he, too, was an enlisted man. He took part in every engagement, and, gun or bayonet in hand, stood ready to "close up" whenever there was a vacancy in the line. The cause of the Confederacy was his, because his master had espoused it first; then it was his from the love he came to bear the flag, and no truer, more loyal heart beat under the gray than that of Amos Rucker.

He joined the Camp of W. H. T. Walker, and there was no more loved nor respected member than the black man, whose bowed form and snow-white hair showed the passing of the years so plainly. He attended every meeting till the one before his death, when he sent word to the camp that he was too ill to attend and added, "Give my love to the boys."

He went to all the reunions whenever possible, and here he attracted much attention. He was very proud to show off a wonderful feat of memory, for he could call the roll of his old company from A to Z, and he would add in solemn tones "here" or "dead" as the names left his lips.

The people who had his lifetime devotion took care of both the old man and his wife. As he said, "My folks give me everything I want."

At his death in Atlanta in August 1909, there was universal sorrow. His body lay in state, and hundreds of both white and black stood with bared head to do him honor. Camp Walker defrayed all burial expenses, buying a lot in the cemetery especially for him, so that the old man and his wife could lie side by side.

The funeral services were conducted by General Clement A. Evans, the commander in chief of the United Confederate Veterans, and his volunteer pallbearers were ex-Governor Allen D. Candler; General A. J. West; ex-Postmaster Amos Fox; F. A. Hilburn, commander of Camp Walker; J. Sid Holland; and R. S. Osbourne. Very tenderly they carried the old veteran to his grave, clothed in his uniform of gray and wrapped in a Confederate flag, a grave made beautiful by flowers from comrades and friends, among which a large design from the Daughters of the Confederacy was conspicuous in its red and white.

A simple monument will be erected to the faithful soldier by the white comrades of his camp and from contributions from his many friends in Atlanta.

Confederate Veteran

"I Want to See Gineral Sherman"

An interesting and unique character that attracted curious attention on the streets here a few days ago was an aged Negro, an ex-slave, who had come all the way from Georgia to have a talk with General Sherman. The old man believed General Sherman was still alive and would be among the survivors of the Grand Army of the Republic assembled in Washington for their fiftieth annual convention.

On arrival at the station he presented a queer figure, arrayed in an age-sleeked broadcloth suit, with a battered silk hat "dat old marster wore befo' de war." On his coat was pinned a small, faded Confederate flag; in one hand he carried a carpetbag and in the other a palmetto cane, on which he leaned heavily.

He paused at the street crossing and with blinking eager eyes stared around nervously, fearing to venture among the traffic, when a policeman came to his rescue.

"Step lively, old man," he said. "You don't seem used to the city, but I'll see you across all right." And he piloted him to a place of safety.

The old Negro took off his hat and almost lost his balance as he made a low bow.

"Thank you, sah; yas, sah, you is right. I was never in a big city befo' or so far from home, but, boss, I'll be might oblige, sah, if you'll show me de procession—de Yankee one I mean—dat Gineral Sherman is likely de head of. I hear tell he's gwine march here today."

"Why, old man, I'm sorry, but you are too late for that. The vets left the city more than a week ago, and the show is over. That's too bad."

"Then pint me to whar I kin find Gineral Sherman, please, sah. I ain't carin' for de parade or de big day. I want to see Gineral Sherman. Is dat whar he lives, in de big white house up yonder?" and with trembling hand he pointed to the Capitol, a short distance away.

The cop restrained a smile as he explained to the old man that General Sherman had been dead many years. . . .

Disappointed, yet with a feeling of duty done, the colored patriarch then unfolded an interesting tale of war days, when he was the bearer of a note from the Yankee leader to a Southern woman, Cecelia Stovall Shelman, who had been the object of Sherman's love before the war. The general had saved her home from destruction during the March to the Sea, and he gave . . . her servant a note which told her he was carrying out his youthful promise of protection.

And so the aged Josiah had come to Washington, where he believed the general was living. . . . "I stood by my white people, long as they lived," he explained, "an' what I come here for was to give the gen'ral the thanks of my mistress."

His duty completed, he has gone back to finish out his last days, a relic of times that were. . . .

Compiled from the
Athens (Ga.) *Daily Herald*
and the
Columbus (Ga.) *Enquirer-Sun*

More Than Kind

For the last fifteen years, a Federal pension of $240 a year, issued to a former Union soldier, has been received regularly at the Confederate Home in Atlanta, Georgia.

Such is the report that comes through a newspaper article sent by a friend, this incident having been disclosed by Colonel R. deT. Lawrence, State Pension Commissioner of Georgia, who has been president of the board of trustees of the home for fourteen years.

The donor is A. H. Wray, of New York, who offered his entire Federal pension to the home with the statement that he did not need it, "and as the boys in blue are well provided for, the money can be put to better use by the boys in gray."

In appreciation of this donation to the needs of the Confederate Home of Georgia, it is planned to pay tribute to this generous foe by placing a plaque, suitably inscribed, in the library of the home, thus to honor one who has shown that he is indeed a friend in peace.

Such actions as this do more to heal the breach between sections than any legislative enactments, for it shows the sympathy which makes us little "less than kin, and more than kind."

Confederate Veteran

Random Acts of Kindness

ACKNOWLEDGMENTS

Like many of the men and women you have just met in the preceding pages, I have relied on the help of friends and the kindness of strangers. First among these is Tom Broadfoot. This book was his idea. During a casual conversation one afternoon, he asked if I would be willing to take on a project he had been thinking about for a long time. I deeply appreciate his trust and sincerely hope he will not be disappointed with the results.

Special thanks also go to Page Gebsen of Broadfoot Publishing. She patiently and skillfully fielded my inquiries about the rank and service of dozens of Confederate soldiers. When questions came up about Union soldiers, Noel Yetter found answers in the National Archives. Duane Burhans also pitched in and took charge of copying and collating scores of pages from dozens of dusty volumes.

At the National Archives, Trevor K. Plante, Michael F. Knight, Terri Hedgpeth, David Wallace, Aloa South, and Wayne DeCesar all went way beyond the call of duty to look up information in pension files, military service records, claims cases, and even in the long forgotten logbook of a Union gunboat.

I also owe a hearty thanks to Ed Raus of the Manassas National Battlefield; Robert Krick of the Fredericksburg National Military Park; Robert E. L. Krick of the Petersburg National Battlefield; Ted Alexander of the Antietam National Battlefield; Stacey Allen of the Shiloh National Military Park; Jim Ogden and Lee White of the Chickamauga National Military Park; Retha Stephens and Willie Ray Johnson of the Kennesaw Mountain National Battlefield Park; Michael Monahan of the U.S. Army Military History Institute; Sergio Velasco of the Texas State Library and Archives; Rosalie Gregg and Sue Tackle of the Wise County (Texas) Heritage Museum; Russell Baker of the Arkansas History Commission; Helen Matthews and Michael Brubaker of the Atlanta History Center; Nelson Morgan, John Wilcox and Marilyn Healey of the University of Georgia Library; and Laura Carter and Freda Fleming of the Athens-Clarke County Library. They all went out of their way to locate information or to track down obscure books and newspapers that helped prove—and sometimes disprove—many of the stories I hoped to use.

Dr. Glenn Robertson of the Combat Studies Institute of the U.S. Army Command and General Staff College cheerfully shared his legendary expertise on the battle of Chickamauga. Civil War historian Scott Patchan shrugged off a bad case of flu to answer questions about the second battle of Bull Run, and Mark Travis, the co-author of a fine regimental history of the 5th New Hampshire Infantry, generously provided me with some of his own detailed research about the battle of Antietam. My friends, Kyle Russell and John Lynch, both took time from their busy schedules to help look into some little known incidents of the Atlanta campaign, while Barry Carson supplied "special research" from the book he knows best.

I am also deeply grateful to Wes Cowan, Dr. and Mrs. Billups P. Tillman, and Dr. and Mrs. Bolling S. DuBose, Jr., for giving me access to private papers and family photographs. In this electronic age, research also relies on computers and websites, and Linda Geiger showed me some new ways to shake a family tree. When the answers to questions about some Masonic mysteries simply led to more questions, Bob Rogers, Sharon and Andy Page, Ron Wolbert of the Zerubbabel Lodge F. & A.M. of Savannah, Georgia, Ray Alvarez of the Grand Lodge F. & A.M. of the State of New York, and Jesse McWilliams of the Grand Lodge F. & A.M. of Alabama all helped put the puzzling pieces together.

A special thanks goes to Lorena Akioka, who has helped me with this project and several others in more ways than I can count. And I cannot say enough about Jean Purvines, Sarah Feldkamp, and Lana Todd of the Lewis County Historical Society in Canton, Missouri. Not once, but twice, these nice ladies drove sixty miles to take pictures in a lonely country cemetery.

The rest of the illustrations in this book would not have been possible without the help and expertise of Katie Brower Gentilello and Frank Hamrick of Photographic Services at the University of Georgia Library, Greg Hirshoren at Campus Graphics and Photography, Mike Winey and Randy Hackenburg at the U.S. Army Military History Institute, and the folks at Northeastern Photo in Harrisburg, Pennsylvania, and King Visual Technology in Hyattsville, Maryland. Their unfailing patience and cheerfulness made the difficult job of putting pictures with stories a whole lot easier. Wendy Giminski, of Campus Graphics and Photography, also worked her special magic to transform my vague ideas into a book cover, while Emily Hardeman, Krysia Haag, and Mark Dodson all offered helpful comments and advice about the design.

I would also like to thank Don Stivers and Don Troiani, two of America's foremost military illustrators. They generously provided the art that graces the cover and 1865 title page of this book.

And last, but certainly not least, is my Mary, who listened to my woes, comforted my sorrows, corrected my mistakes, and *still* loves me best. If that isn't kindness, I don't know what is.

David Evans

Random Acts of Kindness

PICTURE CREDITS

Cover, *"An Act of Compassion,"* by Don Stivers, copyright 1996, Stivers Publishing, used by permission. Cover design by Wendy Giminski. **Page 1,** *Battles and Leaders of the Civil War*, edited by Robert U. Johnson and Clarence C. Buel, vol. 1, p. vi; **Page 16,** Courtesy of Wes Cowan; **Page 23,** *Battles and Leaders of the Civil War*, vol. 2, p. 512; **Page 26,** *Battles and Leaders of the Civil War*, vol. 2, p. 621; **Page 34,** *Confederate Veteran*, vol. 5, p. 281; **Page 40,** *Under Both Flags: A Panorama of the Great Civil War as Represented in Story, Anecdote, Adventure, and the Romance of Reality Written by Celebrities of Both Sides*, p. 198; **Page 46,** *Battles and Leaders of the Civil War*, vol. 1, p. 121; **Page 63,** *Battles and Leaders of the Civil War*, vol. 2, p. 679; **Page 76,** Courtesy of U.S. Army Military History Institute; **Page 82,** Courtesy of Lewis County (Missouri) Historical Society; **Page 83,** *Battles and Leaders of the Civil War*, vol. 3, p. 87; **Page 88,** *Confederate Veteran*, vol. 16, p. 105; **Page 95,** *Thirty Years After: An Artist's Memoir of the Civil War*, by Edwin Forbes, p. 78; **Page 102,** *Southern Bivouac*, vol. 2, p. 333; **Page 113,** *Harper's Weekly*, July 11, 1863, Courtesy of Hargrett Rare Book and Manuscript Library, University of Georgia Libraries; **Page 116,** *Battles and Leaders of the Civil War*, vol. 4, p. 178; **Page 124,** *The Illustrated London News*, June 4, 1864; **Page 138,** *Campfire and Battlefield: A Pictorial Narrative of the Civil War*, by Rossiter Johnson, p. 320; **Page 155,** *Campfire and Battlefield: A Pictorial Narrative of the Civil War*, p. 328; **Page 157,** *Life Studies of the Great Army*, by Edwin Forbes, plate 24, Courtesy of Hargrett Rare Book and Manuscript Library, University of Georgia Libraries; **Page 181,** Courtesy of Dr. and Mrs. Billups P. Tillman; **Page 184,** *Battles and Leaders of the*

Civil War, vol. 3, p. 223; **Page 193,** *Battles and Leaders of the Civil War*, vol. 2, p. 444; **Page 202,** *The Mountain Campaigns of Georgia* (1890 edition), by Joseph M. Brown, p. 65, Courtesy of Hargrett Rare Book and Manuscript Library, University of Georgia Libraries; **Page 215,** Records of the General Accounting Office, Record Group 217, National Archives; **Page 224,** *Battles and Leaders of the Civil War*, vol. 4, p. 320; **Page 234,** *An Unknown Heroine: An Historical Episode of the War Between the States*, by L. E. Chittenden, front piece; **Page 259,** *"From American to American,"* by Don Troiani, copyright 1994, Historical Art Prints, Ltd., used by permission; **Page 278,** *Battles and Leaders of the Civil War*, vol. 4, p. 736; **Page 286,** James Wadsworth Family Papers, Library of Congress; **Page 291,** *Battles and Leaders of the Civil War*, vol. 2, p. 694; **Page 307,** *Campfire and Battlefield: A Pictorial Narrative of the Civil War*, p. 124.

BIBLIOGRAPHY

1861

When Fort Sumter Surrendered: Abner Doubleday, *Reminiscences of Forts Sumter and Moultrie in 1860-61* (New York, Harper & Brothers, 1876), pp. 169-70.

A Heroine in Baltimore: *The Civil War in Song and Story 1860-1865,* ed. Frank Moore (New York: P. F. Collier, 1889), p. 36.

A Chivalrous Soldier: *Confederate Veteran* 25:111-12; U.S. War Department, *The War of the Rebellion: A Compilation of the Official Records of the Union and Confederate Armies* (Washington, D.C.: U.S. Government Printing Office, 1880-1901), series I, vol. 2, p. 655 (hereafter cited as *OR*).

A Woman's Prerogative: J. Albert Monroe, "Reminiscences of the War of the Rebellion of 1861-5," *Military Order of the Loyal Legion of the United States* (hereafter cited as *MOLLUS Papers*) 63 vols. (Wilmington, N.C.: Broadfoot Publishing, 1991-1996), vol. 33, *Personal Narratives of Events in the War of the Rebellion, Being Papers Read before the Rhode Island Soldiers and Sailors Historical Society*, pp. 426-27.

Captured at Wilson's Creek: Otto C. B. Cademann, "A Prisoner of War: A Sequel to the Battle of Wilson's Creek," *MOLLUS Papers*, vol. 49, *War Papers, Being Papers Read before the Commandery of the State of Wisconsin Military Order of the Loyal Legion of the United States*, pp. 439-43.

A Philadelphia Welcome: *The Civil War in Song and Story*, pp. 243-44.

The Old Man and the Private: Henry H. Smith, "General Lee and the Private—A Good War Story," *Camp Fires of the Confederacy*, ed. Ben LaBree (Louisville, Ky.: Courier-Journal Job Printing Company, 1898), pp. 311-13.

1862

Stonewall's Way: George D. Ewing, "Tact of Stonewall Jackson," *Confederate Veteran* 19:412.

The Amenities of War: Sterling Fisher in *Under Both Flags A Panorama of the Great War as Represented in Story, Anecdote, Adventure, and the Romance of Reality, Written by Celebrities of Both Sides; The Men and Woman Who Created the Greatest Epoch of Our Nation's History* (Philadelphia: Fidelity Publishing Company, 1896), pp. 473-75.

On Shiloh's Bloody Field: Wilbur F. Hinman, *The Story of the Sherman Brigade. The Camp, The March, The Bivouac, The Battle; and How "The Boys" Lived and Died During Four Years of Active Field Service* (By the Author: 1897), pp. 147-48.

He Was a Child: Lovell H. Rousseau in *The Rebellion Record, A Diary of American Events with Documents, Narratives, Illustrative Incidents, Poetry, etc.,* ed. Frank Moore, 11 vols. (New York: G. P. Putnam, 1861-1863; D. Van Nostrand, 1864-1869), 6:10.

As You Sow: C. W. Boyce, "A Story of the Shenandoah Valley in 1862," *Under Both Flags*, pp. 198-203.

He Found Her Boy: Dr. Hunter H. McGuire, "General Thomas J. Jackson," *Southern Historical Society Papers* 19:308-9.

An Incident of the Battle of Malvern Hill: "A Rabbit in a Battle—An Incident of the Battle-Field of Malvern Hill," *Augusta* (Ga.) *Chronicle & Sentinel*, October 3, 1862, p. 2.

The Last Full Measure: James Tanner, "Corporal Tanner's Unparalleled Experience," *Camp-Fire Sketches and Battle-Field Echoes of the Rebellion,* ed. W. C. King and W. P. Derby, (Springfield, Mass.: King, Richardson & Company, 1888), pp. 278-80.

An Act of Kindness Goes Awry: Henry B. Freeman, "Eighteenth U. S. Infantry From Camp Thomas to Murfreesboro and the Regular Brigade at Stone River," *MOLLUS Papers*, vol. 28, *Glimpses of the Nations Struggle, Papers Read Before the Minnesota Commandery of the Military Order of the Loyal Legion of the United States, 1889-1892*, pp.117-19.

The Price of Freedom: Ulysses R. Brooks, "War Memories," *Confederate Veteran* 22:497-98.

Lincoln and the Colonel: Moses Veal, "With Malice Toward None; With Charity for All," *MOLLUS Papers*, vol. 59, *Military Essays of the Pennsylvania Commandery Military Order of the Loyal Legion of the United States*, p. 107.

General Lee's Consideration for His Soldiers: Theodore Hartman, *Confederate Veteran* 30:45.

A Masonic Incident: J. Madison Drake, "Freemasonry the Strongest Fraternal Tie," *Confederate Veteran* 22:129.

Clara Barton on the Battlefield: James L. Dunn in *The Civil War in Song and Story*, p. 244-45.

A Little Girl's Kindness to the Soldiers: *The Civil War in Song and Story*, p. 181.

Homecoming for a Confederate: Henry Kyd Douglas quoted by John L. Smith, *History of the Corn Exchange Regiment 118th Pennsylvania Volunteers, from their first engagement at Antietam to Appomattox* (Philadelphia: J. L. Smith, 1888), pp. 91-94.

Arkansas Soldiers in Virginia: Alexander C. Jones, *Confederate Veteran* 20:464.

When Duty Demanded Disobedience: Smith, *History of the Corn Exchange Regiment 118th Pennsylvania Volunteers*, pp. 76-78.

Greater Love Hath No Man: *Confederate Veteran* 25:155-56.

Buck's Baby: Robert Stiles, *Four Years Under Marse Robert* (New York and Washington: The Neale Publishing Company, 1903), pp. 130-31.

The Angel of Marye's Heights: Joseph B. Kershaw, "No More 'A Nameless Hero.' A Worthy Tribute to Sergeant Richard Kirkland," *Charleston News and Courier*, February 6, 1880.

A Confederate Christmas: Janet H. Weaver Randolph, *Confederate Veteran* 13:572.

Kindness of General Jeff C. Davis: William H. McCauley, *Confederate Veteran* 10:72.

1863

Going Home: *New York Herald*, quoted by *Mobile Advertiser and Register*, January 24, 1863, p. 1.

Modesty Becomes Her: William A. Campbell, "A Friend in Need," *Confederate Veteran* 11:291.

Mrs. Sarah Bell Waller: W. O. G., *The Southern Bivouac*, March 1884, pp. 333-36.

The Good Georgia Governor: *Augusta* (Ga.) *Daily Constitutionalist*, March 4, 1863, p. 1.

Generous Action of a Comrade: Claudine Rhett, *Confederate Veteran* 3:7.

The Episode of Patrick Conley: Rev. John F. Moors, "The Episode of Patrick Connolly," *Camp-Fire Sketches and Battle-Field Echoes of the Rebellion*, pp. 173-74.

An Incident at Vicksburg: William S. Forbes, "Recollections of General Grant During the Siege of Vicksburg," *MOLLUS Papers*, vol. 59, *Military Essays of the Pennsylvania Commandery Military Order of the Loyal Legion of the United States*, pp. 23-25.

General Grant and the Teamster: Jacob W. Wilkin, "Vicksburg," *MOLLUS Papers*, vol. 13, *Military Essays and*

Recollections, Papers Read Before the Commandery of the State of Illinois, Military Order of the Loyal Legion of the United States, p. 233.

They Were So Hungry: Wilbur F. Phares, "Soldier Gave His Flour to Woman and Children," *Confederate Veteran* 16:18.

"I Am the Man, Sir": John B. Gordon, *Reminiscences of the Civil War* (New York: Charles Scribner's Sons, 1904), pp. 150-53.

On the Field at Gettysburg: A. L. Long, *Memoirs of General Robert E. Lee: His Military and Personal History Embracing a Large Amount of Information Hitherto Unpublished* (New York, Philadelphia, and Washington: J. M. Stoddart & Company, 1886), pp. 301-302.

Lee's Regard for Private Property: D. L. Sublett, *Confederate Veteran* 4:401.

An Act of Mercy: John Wesley Dixon, *Confederate Veteran* 40:142-43.

"I Have Never Forgotten You": Mrs. W. D. Chadick, "Civil War Days in Huntsville, A Diary of Mrs. W. D. Chadick," *Alabama Historical Quarterly* 9 (Summer 1947):230-33.

How Confederates Treated a Federal: William C. Brown, *Confederate Veteran* 13:228.

My Johnnie Friend: Harmon M. Billings, "A Yank Seeks the Address of a Johnnie," *Confederate Veteran* 12:177.

"It's All I Can Do": William Abbott, "My Escape from Belle Isle," *MOLLUS Papers,* vol. 50, *War Papers, Being Papers Read Before the Commandery of the State of Michigan Military Order of the Loyal Legion of the United States,* pp. 243-53.

Bunny: Fannie A. Beers, *The Southern Bivouac,* February 1884, pp. 264-66.

A Pair of Mittens: Alexander Belcher, *The Southern Bivouac,* April 1884, p. 378.

Down in Tennessee: S. H. Stout, *Confederate Veteran* 16:18-19.
In Winter Quarters at Dalton, Georgia: James H. M'Neilly, *Confederate Veteran* 28:131.
Number 27 and the Pumpkin Pie: "Pumpkin Pie for a Sick Yankee," *Chicago Times-Herald*, quoted by *Confederate Veteran* 5:575-76.

1864

Kentucky Confederates in Kokomo: Ed Porter Thompson, *History of the Orphan Brigade* (Louisville, Ky.: Lewis N. Thompson, 1898), pp. 947-48.
Ties That Bind: Andrew Johnston, "A Correction of the Incident in Reference to General Pickett," *Southern Historical Society Papers* 1:387-88; *OR*, series II, vol. 6, pp. 993-94, 1093.
"It Will Just Ruin Our Honor": Gordon, *Reminiscences of the Civil War*, pp. 110-12.
General Forrest Among Civilians: Charles W. Anderson, *Confederate Veteran* 3:106.
A Young Lady of Tuscaloosa: William L. Truman, *Confederate Veteran* 17:60.
"You Should Have Some Feeling": Walter B. Barker, "Two Anecdotes of General Lee," *Southern Historical Society Papers* 12:328-29.
Professional Courtesy: "Treatment of Prisoners," *Confederate Veteran* 3:297; *OR*, series II, vol. 7, p. 135.
Praying With a Dying Enemy: Stiles, *Four Years Under Marse Robert*, pp. 255-56.
Sherman and "Miss Cecelia": Maggie Thornton, "Romance of Sherman in Cherokee Georgia," *Chattanooga Times*, no date.
Dividing the Spoils: W. H. Lee, "'Johnnie' and 'Yank' Divide the Hog," *Confederate Veteran* 17:342.

Strange Bedfellows: I. E. Kellie, "Why I Got in Bed with a Corpse," *Confederate Veteran* 14:361-62.

A Friend in Need: Frank Wilkeson, *Recollections of a Private Soldier in the Army of the Poto*mac (New York: G. P. Putnam's Sons, 1887), pp. 135-38.

Standing on the Promises: Emily V. Mason, "Hospital Scenes," *Our Women in the War. The Lives They Lived; The Deaths They Died,* ed. *Charleston Weekly News and Courier* (Charleston, S.C.: News and Courier Book Presses, 1885), pp. 148-50.

Compassion for a Confederate: George H. Blakeslee, "Pathetic Tribute from a Federal," *Confederate Veteran* 5:475-76.

An Incident at Kennesaw Mountain: W. T. Barnes, "An Incident of Kennesaw Mountain," *Confederate Veteran* 30:48-49.

Unconscious with Kindness: Alfred J. Vaughan, Jr., "A Few Incidents," *Camp Fires of the Confederacy*, pp. 67-69.

Master and Slave: Samuel Coleman, "Master and His Faithful Slave," *Confederate Veteran* 20:410.

A Night on the Battlefield: *The Women of the South in War Times,* comp. Matthew Page Andrews, (Baltimore: The Norman, Remington Company, 1920), pp. 145-47.

Turning the Other Cheek: P. H. Hesterly, Southern Claims Commission Case Number 6,560, Record Group 217, Records of the General Accounting Office, National Archives, Washington, D.C.

Pity on a Prisoner: W. J. W. Kerr, "Sad Ending of a Wedding Trip," *Confederate Veteran* 23:318.

At the Battle of Mobile Bay: William F. Hutchinson, "The Bay Fight: A Sketch of the Battle of Mobile Bay, August 5th, 1864," *MOLLUS Papers*, vol. 32, *Personal Narratives of Events in the War of the Rebellion, Being Papers Read Before the Rhode Island Soldiers and Sailors Historical Society*, pp. 231-32.

Born in Battle: Fifteenth Corps, "Born In Battle: How Gen.

Logan Became Godfather to the Fatherless—A True Story That is Stranger Than Fiction," *Washington Bulletin*, quoted by *Pittsburgh Reveille*, July 16, 1884.

Mrs. McPeek: *Atlanta Constitution*, quoted by *Southern Historical Society Papers* 23:328-29; Alley McPeek, Southern Claims Commission Case Number 1,028, Record Group 217, Records of the General Accounting Office, National Archives, Washington, D.C.

A Rebel Heroine: Aldace F. Walker in *MOLLUS Papers*, vol.13, *Military Essays and Recollections, Papers Read Before the Commandery of the State of Illinois, Military Order of the Loyal Legion of the United States*, pp. 416-29.

An Incident of a Sword: Nathaniel Ingraham Hasell, *Confederate Veteran* 20:159.

Caring for a Wounded Enemy: E. H. Matthews, *Confederate Veteran* 11:163-64.

Only a Private: *Detroit Free Press*, quoted by *The Southern Bivouac*, May 1885, p. 422.

On the March to the Sea: Charles E. Belknap, "Recollections of a Bummer," *MOLLUS Papers*, vol. 43, *War Papers, Being Papers Read Before the Commandery of the District of Columbia Military Order of the Loyal Legion of the United States*, pp. 20-22.

Two Unknown Heroes: Charles H. Olmstead, "Two 'Unknown Heroes' of the Ranks," *Southern Historical Society Papers* 11:139-40.

"Let Me Show You": William A. Obenchain, "How Gen. Lee Made Glad the Heart of a Subaltern," *Confederate Veteran* 9:224.

"Mother, Don't You Worry": James F. Rusling, "Abraham Lincoln and His Religious Faith," *MOLLUS Papers*, vol. 59, *Military Essays of the Pennsylvania Commandery Military Order of the Loyal Legion of the United States*, pp. 428-30.

1865

How I Lost and Recovered My Hat: John William Jones, *Confederate Veteran* 11:458.

A Case of Mistaken Identity: James T. Lambright, "Yankees Taken for Rebels at Columbia," *Confederate Veteran* 18:158.

With Sherman in South Carolina: Frank H. Putney, "Incidents of Sherman's March Through the Carolinas," *MOLLUS Papers*, vol. 48, *War Papers, Being Papers Read before the Commandery of the State of Wisconsin Military Order of the Loyal Legion of the United States*, pp. 381, 384-86.

Who Is Thy Neighbor?: James M. Emery, *Confederate Veteran* 19:339.

A Generous Enemy: J. D. Hodges, *Confederate Veteran* 21:495.

"That Was My Brother": Charles H. T. Collis, "Lincoln's Magnanimity," quoted in Septima M. Collis, *A Woman's War Record* (New York and London: G. P. Putnam's Sons, 1889), pp. 61-70.

At Appomattox: Horace Porter, *Campaigning with Grant* (New York: The Century Company, 1897), pp. 475-80.

Washington City on the Night of Mr. Lincoln's Assassination: Cornelius Tacitus Allen, "Sixteen Years Ago—Washington City on the Night of Mr. Lincoln's Assassination," *Princeton* (Ky.) *Banner*, quoted by *The Southern Bivouac*, September 1882, pp. 18-22.

Lincoln's Legacy: Grenville M. Dodge, "Personal Recollections of Some of Our Great Commanders in the Civil War," *MOLLUS Papers*, vol. 22, *Personal Recollections of the War of the Rebellion, Addresses Delivered Before the Commander of the State of New York, Military Order of the Loyal Legion of the United States*, pp. 210-11.

1865 & Beyond

How a Confederate Got Home in 1865: John T. Bowden, *Confederate Veteran* 17:58-59.

A Moment's Contemplation: J. J. Kane, quoted in *Confederate Veteran* 1:145.

How Grant Saved Lee: Franklin H. Barroll in *Camp-Fire Sketches and Battle-Field Echoes of the Rebellion*, pp. 302-303.

I Had Been Her Slave: Jerry W. May, "Jerry May Got His Old Mistress a Pension," *Confederate Veteran* 13:423.

Amos Rucker, Negro Veteran: *Confederate Veteran* 17:496.

"I Want to See Gineral Sherman": "Ex-Slave Was Looking for General Sherman," *Athens* (Ga.) *Daily Herald*, March 20, 1916; "Thanks for Sherman Arrrive Too Late," *Columbus* (Ga.) *Enquirer-Sun*, October 29, 1915.

More Than Kind: "A Generous Foe," *Confederate Veteran* 38:331.

Index

IOWA TROOPS:
  5th Iowa Cavalry 214
  8th Iowa Cavalry 184
Irish Bend, LA, Battle of 108
Ironton, OH 296
Island Number 10, Mississippi River,
  Battle of 103
Iuka, MS 53
Iuka, MS, Battle of 30, 185
Ivor Station, VA 161

J

Jack, Uncle (slave) 144, 145
Jackson, LA, Battle of 126
Jackson, MS 268
Jackson, Thomas J. (Stonewall),
  Lieutenant General 20, 25–26
  39, 46–47, 70, 71, 72
Jackson, TN 167
Jackson, William H., Brigadier
  General 185
James River 273, 282
Jay's Mill, Chickamauga, GA 132
Jeffersonville, IN 159
John (7th NJ Infantry) 256–258
Johnson, William P., Colonel 297
Johnson's Island, Lake Erie 287
Johnston, Joseph E., General 185,
  206, 293, 296
Jones, Alexander C., Captain 74
Jones, Bill 160
Jones Farm, VA, Battle of 243
Jones, John William, Chaplain 261–
  262
Jonesboro, GA 226, 227
Jonesboro, GA, Battle of 226
Judkins, Tommy 207, 208

K

Kane, J. J., Ensign 297–298

Kellie, I. E., Private 185–189
Kennedy, J. D., Captain 86
Kennesaw Mountain, GA 197
Kennesaw Mountain, GA, Battle of
  200–203, 204
KENTUCKY TROOPS (Confederate):
  1st Kentucky Cavalry 160
  2nd Kentucky Infantry 38
  4th Kentucky Cavalry 27
KENTUCKY TROOPS (Union):
  26th Kentucky Infantry 294
Kerr, W. J. W. 216–218
Kershaw County, SC 86
Kershaw, Joseph B., Brigadier
  General 86, 87, 88, 98
Keyser, Elizabeth. *See* Van Metrie,
  Bettie, Mrs.
Kilpatrick, Judson, Brigadier General
  263
Kirby, William M., Lieutenant 161
Kirkland, John 86
Kirkland, Richard, Sergeant 86-88
Knoxville, TN 247
Kokomo, IN 159–160

L

Lackawanna (U.S. ship) 219
Lambright, James T., Private 263–
  264
Lane, James H., Brigadier General
  243
Lawrence, R. deT. 306
Lawton, Alexander R., Brigadier
  General 97
Lawton, Edward P., Captain 97–98
Lawton, Edward P., Mrs. 97–98
Lebanon, MO 15
Lee, George Washington Custis,
  Major General 272